THE
USA

Horrible Histories:
The Savage Stone Age
The Awesome Egyptians
The Groovy Greeks
The Rotten Romans
The Cut-throat Celts
The Smashing Saxons
The Vicious Vikings
The Angry Aztecs
The Incredible Incas
The Stormin' Normans
The Measly Middle Ages
The Terrible Tudors
Even More Terrible Tudors
The Slimy Stuarts
The Gorgeous Georgians
The Vile Victorians
The Frightful First World War
The Woeful Second World War
The Blitzed Brits

Horrible Histories Specials:
Bloody Scotland
Cruel Kings and Mean Queens
Dark Knights and Dingy Castles
Ireland
Rowdy Revolutions
The 20th Century
Wicked Words

Also available:
Dreadful Diary
Horrible Christmas
The Horribly Huge Quiz Book
Loathsome Letter-writing Pack
The Mad Millennium Play

THE
USA

TERRY DEARY
ILLUSTRATED BY MARTIN BROWN

SCHOLASTIC

For Andrew Amies-Rudd, a Horrible Histories fan and a boy with a lot of heart. An inspiration.

Scholastic Children's Books,
Commonwealth House, 1–19 New Oxford Street
London WC1A 1NU, UK

A division of Scholastic Ltd
London ~ New York ~ Toronto ~ Sydney ~ Auckland
Mexico City ~ New Delhi ~ Hong Kong

Published in the UK by Scholastic Ltd, 2001

ISBN 0 439 99939 1

CONTENTS

INTRODUCTION

History can be horrible ... but some places can give us more horrible history than others! Take the United States of America, for example.

As US Vice-President Al Gore said in October 2000...

Yes, we've made mistakes in the past ... but, by God, we're the greatest country on the face of this Earth – we always have been, we always will be!

Modest Al! A lot of Americans BELIEVED him and (almost) made him their 43rd president.

But this is a Horrible History. So we'll be taking a look at those little 'mistakes' the USA made in the past.

This wonderful nation has given us the joys of...

And they're just the good things about the USA!

The greatest country on the face of this earth has also led the way in giving us:

- nuclear weapons to wipe us all out 50 times over
- massive pollution to wipe us all out a bit slower.

But some of the worst things are their history books! The US school books have fat fibs about American heroes like…

What we need is a Horrible History of the USA that tells it the way it *really* was. And, as it happens, you are reading one right now!

HORRIBLE HISTORIES HEALTH WARNING:
Do not read this while eating a burger and Coke. Some of these savage stories are so gruesomely gory you may throw up. And this book is too good to be spoiled by your vomit!

CRUEL COLUMBUS

The date everyone remembers is…

IN FOURTEEN-HUNDRED AND NINETY-TWO COLUMBUS SAILED THE OCEAN BLUE

But Chris Columbus was probably the worst thing ever to happen to the land we call America. Forget those stories that he was an explorer, setting off to prove the world was round – in 1492 most people knew that because you could see it when a ship disappeared over the horizon. No, Chris was after one thing – wealth.

Chris and his Spanish masters wanted gold, land, gold, slaves and gold. That's what they got. The land and the gold belonged to the native 'Indians', of course, but that didn't matter to the savage Spanish. The invasion cost Chris very little – it cost the Indians he met everything.

Cruel Columbus timeline

28,000 BC That's before even your teacher was born. First humans arrive in North America from Asia.

AD 982 Viking 'Eric the Red' discovers Greenland and Vikings almost certainly reach America.

1492 Along comes Christopher Columbus to 'discover' America – though the native people had never lost it.

HAVE WE MET BEFORE?

1504 Sailor Amerigo Vespucci visits the 'New World'. Letters say he 'discovered' it. A map-maker believes the letters and names the New World 'America' after 'Amerigo'. The name catches on!

1587 English Queen Elizabeth sends settlers to claim land in North America. 114 land at Roanoke – 114 disappear, never to be seen again.

Terrible text books

Everyone knows Cruel Chris Columbus (CCC) was an Italian who discovered America for the Spanish ... but was he? That's one of the 'facts' that many historians argue about. There are quite a few about the mysterious Mr C...

...or maybe Spain ... or maybe Portugal ... or maybe Corsica. No one can agree. (*Horrible Histories* can state for certain he was *not* born in all four.)

...or a rich weaver. (Depends on which book you read.)

…except that's just a fairy story that never happened.

…except none of that is true!

Date and place true but nothing else – the Vikings almost certainly reached North America 500 years before him! CCC always believed he had landed in Asia (or 'the Indies' as it was known) and that's why he called the natives 'Indians'.

Poppycock! He died wealthy with the title 'Admiral of the Ocean Sea'.

Cruel Chris Columbus

Why don't school books tell you the truth? Because they want you to believe nice fairy tales. Here are a few foul facts about Cruel Chris Columbus...

1 Greedy Chris
By 13 October CCC's diary already shows his true colours...

> At daybreak great multitudes of men came to the shore. I listened very carefully to them and tried to find out if they had any gold. I gathered from their signs that if I sailed south I would find a king with great cups full of gold. I could conquer all of these people with just fifty men and rule them as I please.

2 Slaver Chris

When CCC set off for home he kidnapped around 20 Indians. The terrible conditions on the ships meant only seven arrived in Spain alive. They were enough to show the Spanish that these strong Indians would make great slaves.

CCC headed back to the New World – and this time he had over 1,200 soldiers armed with guns, swords, cannon and attack dogs. And he wasn't going for a holiday – Disney World hadn't been invented. He was going back for more slaves.

In 1495 the Spanish rounded up 500 Arawak Indians on Haiti to be sent back to Spain and took another 500 to work for them on the islands. Half the slaves died on the journey but CCC shrugged and said...

> *Although they die now they will not always die. We can send all the slaves from here that you can sell!*

But he was wrong. Forced work and dreadful diseases would eventually kill off all the Arawaks!

3 Trendy Chris

Chris set a fashion for turning natives into slaves. By 1516 the Spanish on Haiti had killed off most of the Arawaks and they were having to bring in slaves from other American Indian lands.

Slaves were packed into ships like sardines on supermarket shelves. They were locked in to stop them escaping and died in the filthy, scorching air. Spanish history writer Peter Martyr said you didn't need a compass to find your way along the slave ship routes...

All you had to do was follow the trail of dead Indians that had to be thrown overboard.

When the Spaniards ran out of slaves they started capturing them in Africa and taking them across the Atlantic to work there. CCC began the terrible slave trade that lasted another 400 years.

4 Lord Chris

The Spanish forced the Arawaks to obey them. Every now and then they packed a fresh batch off to Spain as slaves. A Spaniard said…

When we went to round up the Arawaks there were many women with babies in their arms. The women were so afraid they left the babies on the ground and ran away.

Your mum wouldn't do that … would she?

The Arawaks who escaped were hunted down for fun and killed.

Quick quiz

What use was a dead Arawak to a Spaniard?

a) The corpses were fed to the Spanish dogs.

b) They were stood in fields as scarecrows.

c) They were thrown on fires as fuel.

Answer: a)

5 Cruel Chris

CCC went back to Haiti in 1493 and forced the Indians to work for the Spanish. They had to grow food, dig for gold or spin cotton.

The Indians weren't allowed to say no and an Indian who disobeyed would have their nose cut off or their ears lopped. They'd be sent back to the village as a warning to the others:

And you think your school punishments are bad!

6 Record-breaker Chris

CCC made a fortune in gold for his Spanish lords and a fair bit for himself. He may not hold the record as the first European on American soil but he probably has a much nastier record: CCC probably sent more Indian slaves to Spain than any other single person.

And the Arawaks who stayed on Haiti became slaves too. CCC's system was simple…

15

> YOU WILL EACH PAY ME IN GOLD, COTTON OR FOOD. YOU WILL PAY EVERY THREE MONTHS. IN RETURN I WILL GIVE YOU A COPPER TOKEN THAT YOU WILL WEAR AROUND YOUR NECK. ANY MAN OR WOMAN CAUGHT WITHOUT A TOKEN WILL IMMEDIATELY HAVE A HAND CUT OFF. FAIR ENOUGH?

The Arawaks spent so much time earning their tokens they hadn't time to feed their families.

Foul fact: The Indians soon grew so desperate they couldn't stand living with CCC and his friends any longer. Many killed themselves – by hanging, poison or throwing themselves on to sharpened wood stakes.

Fouler fact: Sometimes a hundred at a time jumped off a cliff.

Foulest fact: Many mothers killed their children to save the kids from a life of misery.

> CLUB OR COLUMBUS?

> I'LL HAVE THE CLUB PLEASE MUMMY

7 Warrior Chris

CCC was a great fighter – but only when he was fighting against people without cannon, swords or horses.

When the Arawaks tried to fight back in 1495, CCC sent heavily armed soldiers to mow them down. CCC had a son,

Ferdinand, who wrote about his dreadful dad and said he used an even more terrible weapon against the Indians...

The most terrible weapons were the twenty attack dogs who immediately tore the Indians apart. These animals ripped open the limbs and bellies and chased fleeing Indians into the bush.

The Indians who were captured alive were simply killed.

Foul fact: In later years these dogs were used to hunt Indians just for sport, the way people with beanbag brains hunt deer today.

8 Cheating Chris

CCC wanted everyone to believe that he had done what he set out to do – sailed west to find Japan in the east. He made his men swear an oath...

I swear by Almighty God that we have landed near Japan. If this is a lie may I have my tongue cut out of my head!

So it wasn't only the poor American Indians who suffered Chris's cruelty!

Final foul fact: There were around two million Arawaks on the West Indian islands of Greater Antilles when CCC arrived in 1492. Sixty years later there were none.

SAVAGE SETTLERS

After Christopher Columbus, the Pilgrim Fathers (and the other settlers from Europe) were the next-worst thing to happen to the American Indians. The savage settlers took the Indians' land and gave them only disease and misery.

Savage settlers timeline

1607 English settlers set up in Jamestown, Virginia, to start a new life – robbing the country of its riches.
1616 'The Virgin Soil Epidemic'. Diseases like measles from Europe wipe out millions of Native Americans. Only one in ten left. Hard to spot the measles survivors.
1619 First African slaves sent to North America.
1620 Pilgrims run away from England and settle in Patuxet – but call it Plymouth 'cos it reminds them of home sweet home.
1620s Settlers from Europe discover this North America is a good place to grow tobacco – and grow rich! It's going to be hard to get rid of them now.
1664 The Brits arrive at the Dutch colony of New Amsterdam, pinch it from them and change the name to New York.
1675 King Philip's War – the Wampanoag tribe's chief's son (nicknamed King Philip) tries to rebel against settlers in New

England. Settlers massacred, Indians massacred back.

1739 Black slaves of South Carolina rebel by simply walking off to Spanish Florida and freedom. They kill 21 white people they meet on the way. But when they meet an army of white settlers the rebels are massacred.

1750s The Brits claim the east of America, the French the middle and the Spanish the west. This is bound to lead to trouble. In 1754 George Washington goes to battle against the French. Good practice for later...

1762 Now Spain joins in to bash the Brits! Two against one! A year later a peace treaty leaves Spain with the west ... and France with nothing! The Indians (squashed in the middle) are promised that the Brits won't move west to take their lands. Believe that if you like!

The vile Virginians

Many people think a group called the 'Pilgrim Fathers' were the first savage settlers from northern Europe. They weren't. There was a British colony set up ten years before in Virginia who went there to plunder the 'new' land. Here are some facts about them...

1 The Virginia invaders dug for gold in Jamestown instead of digging to plant crops. Of course they began to starve. In the winter of 1609 came the 'Starving Time'.

English settler, George Percy, wrote some disgusting descriptions of their sufferings…

We were driven, through hunger to eat things it is not natural to eat. We ate the flesh and the excrement of man. As well as our own people we ate an Indian after he had been buried for three days. We ate him all.

Imagine eating 'excrement' … that's poo, if you didn't know!

DO YOU HAVE ANYTHING OTHER THAN ROTTING HUMAN FLESH?

POO PORRIDGE, POO PANCAKE, POO PATTIES, POO PASTY, POO PIZZA, POO PATÉ, POO PIE AND POO PUDDING

I'LL HAVE THE ROTTING HUMAN FLESH

2 After that some of the other tasty treats they ate must have seemed gorgeous! They ate dogs, rats, mice, snakes and horses.

WHAT'S THIS?

MICE CRISPIES!

CRUNCH CRUNCH

3 Don't tell your dad about this Virginian horror: a man killed his wife and began to eat her! He had begun to preserve her in salt (so she'd get him through the winter) when he was caught! The man was hanged ... but not eaten.

4 To add to their misery the Jamestown settlers fell ill. They suffered diseases like dysentery (where they had bloody poo) and one man died after...

The problem is that the water they were drinking was unhealthy stuff. George Percy said...

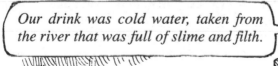

Our drink was cold water, taken from the river that was full of slime and filth.

It could be that they were drinking the water too close to the spot where their toilets drained into.

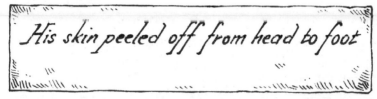

5 Life was tough for those early Virginia settlers – or 'Planters' as they called themselves. Between 1606 and 1625, 7,289 Planters landed and 6,040 of them were soon 'planted' in the ground, dead. Starvation, disease and Indian attacks killed them off.

Planter Richard Frethorne wrote…

I didn't know a head could hold as much water as that which flows from my eyes every day!

He was dead within a year of writing that.

6 In 2000 a scientist came up with a new idea. The Planters at Jamestown didn't die of hunger and disease. They died of poisoning!

The English and the Spanish hated one another and the Spanish didn't want the English in America. A war would have cost a lot of money. It was much easier to simply send a spy into the Jamestown settlement and poison the food or drink.

Arsenic would be the easiest poison to use. It has no taste or smell and there was a lot of it in Jamestown in the Planters' day. They used it to kill rats. Did someone use it to kill them?

SERVES THEM RIGHT

7 The Planters couldn't do much about the diseases, they *could* have been better farmers and they certainly could have made peace with the Indians ... but they weren't very good at it.

The Planters made a deal with the Indians on the Potomac river, a deal that meant 'friendship for life'. The Virginians kept to the deal easily ... because they made sure the 'life' of the Indians was very short.

'Join us in a drink!' the Virginians offered.

The Indians drank the Planters' special ale ... but the Planters didn't drink it. The Indian chief, his family and 200 of his tribe dropped dead from poison. Vicious Virginians!

8 But the Indians could be guilty of cruelty and treachery too. Chief Opechancanough sent a peace party to talk to the Planters. They ate breakfast together, then the Indians grabbed whatever weapons they could find and slaughtered every man, woman and child they could catch! They killed 350 Planters when there were only about 1,000 in the whole of Virginia.

Twenty-two years later Chief Opechancanough said to the Planters, 'Why don't I send a peace party to talk with you?'

What would you have done if you'd been a settler? Said, 'No thanks, Ope, old chap!'?

The settlers said, 'Yes.'

What did Opechancanough's peace party do? They massacred over 300 of them again.

23

The Pilgrim Fathers

These people didn't like the English Church so they moved to Holland. They didn't like the Dutch so they packed up and set sail for America. They didn't seem to like much, did they?

Here's a quick question for your maths teacher…

They landed – on Boxing Day, 1620 on the north-east coast – to 'settle', but they don't seem to have thought about this 'settling' lark. Pilgrim William Mullins took 126 pairs of shoes and 13 pairs of boots but NO ONE took a plough or a horse, a cow or even a fishing line.

The Indians they met helped them survive.

The trouble is the pilgrims DID take some nasty little friends with them … diseases. The Indians had never met these diseases before, their bodies weren't protected against them, and so they were killed off by the million.

What a way to thank the people who saved you! And what's more, the Indian deaths made it easy for the 'settlers' to spread till they took over the continent.

The Indians had cleared the forests and learned to plant corn and built villages. The Pilgrim Fathers moved on to the cleared land and then…

● They stole from the villages. A Pilgrim wrote…

> The sailors had their guns and heard nobody so they entered the houses. They found the people were gone. The sailors took some things but didn't dare stay. We meant to leave some beads in the houses but we didn't do it because we left in such a hurry.

Hah! A likely story! A bit like a burglar pinching your video recorder, then saying, 'I was going to leave you some cash but I heard the cops coming and made a run for it!'

- They stole from the Indian grain stores…

> We marched to a place called Cornhill where we had found corn once before. We dug and found three baskets full and a bag of beans, which will be enough. It was with God's help that we found this corn.

Even better! That's a bit like the burglar saying, 'I found your house empty and the door open so God must have wanted me to rob you!'

- Worst of all they robbed Indian graves…

> We found a place like a grave. We decided to dig it up. We found a mat, a fine bow, bowls, dishes and trays. We took several of the prettiest things to carry away with us and covered up the body again.

How gruesome can you get? Our burglar says, 'I went off and stole from your granny's grave – but it's all right because I covered up her corpse again!' Grim pilgrims.

Did you know…?

The early settlers were religious people. They believed in 'obedience' … especially for the kids. In 1648 a law was passed in Massachusetts which said…

> A young person must not strike a parent or swear at them. Any one over the age of sixteen who swears at or strikes a parent will be put to death.

And you thought your school rules were tough!

In fact there are no records of anyone actually being executed for muttering murderous words at mum or flattening father.

New England – old cruelty

The Indians in the south had suffered under Columbus and the Spanish armies. The tribes in the north were soon suffering too once the English arrived.

In King Philip's War in 1675 a soldier's report says…

The Indian was ordered to be torn to pieces by dogs, and so she was.

GRRRR

Not an unusual fate! William Bradford described an attack on an Indian village where most of the victims were women and children. He reported…

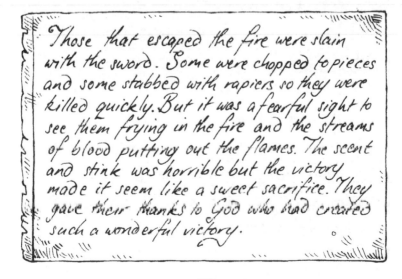

Those that escaped the fire were slain with the sword. Some were chopped to pieces and some stabbed with rapiers so they were killed quickly. But it was a fearful sight to see them frying in the fire and the streams of blood putting out the flames. The scent and stink was horrible but the victory made it seem like a sweet sacrifice. They gave their thanks to God who had created such a wonderful victory.

King Philip was captured and his head was stuck on a pole. (They probably thought God would enjoy that too!)

King Philip's son was the grandson of the chief who had saved the Pilgrims in 1620 ... so they spared him. They 'only' sent him to be a slave in the West Indies.

When five Indian chiefs came to talk peace they met John Washington, an ancestor of America's first President. The settlers didn't get what they wanted, so they killed the chiefs.

Is that *your* idea of peace talks?

Dutch treat

It wasn't only the English who treated the Indians harshly. The Dutch settlers in New Amsterdam could be pretty bloodthirsty too. If a Dutch settler had written a letter about their massacre of the Wappinger Indians then it might have looked like this – the facts are all horribly true...

Dear Meindert

I hope this letter finds you well. In fact I hope this letter finds you at all! The Atlantic is deep and wide and things get lost.

Anyway, the last time I wrote I told you about the Dutch farmer who was murdered. We weren't sure who killed the man but we settlers were talking about Indians. We told the governor that we wanted revenge — or he would be sacked! So the governor allowed us to take our revenge.

Of course we couldn't go running around looking for Indians to kill. That would be too dangerous! They could kill us! So instead we picked on the Wappinger tribe because they were handy. A few weeks ago the Wappingers came to us asking us to shelter them. We gave them shelter and we gave them food and they are nice, friendly, harmless people.

But they are Indians.

And we wanted to kill Indians. So we wiped out the Wappingers!

Of course we didn't want to fight them in battle because someone may have got hurt! So we waited till they were all asleep. The men ran into the Wappinger shelter and massacred every man, woman and child they could find. They quickly lopped off their heads and stuck them on poles so the world could see what we Dutch do when one of our farmers is killed!

One of the heads fell off its pole and Mrs Cuyp ran and kicked it all the way down the street. It made good sport to watch, even though the blood and brains splattered out and ruined her skirts!

Only one Wappinger was left alive because he'd been out of the shelter when the Wappingers were exterminated. He got the worst treatment of all. I almost felt sorry for him!

First the men held him down and cut off his naughty bits - you know the bits I mean, Meindert? Then they sliced off his skin, cut off pieces of flesh and forced him to eat his own flesh. When the governor saw this he thought it was hilarious! He laughed till tears ran down his face. I wish you'd been here to see it, Meindert! You would have enjoyed it. I am off now to play this new sport of kicking a head around the street.

Your dear friend,   Jacob

The letter is made up. But all those awful incidents really did happen.

Scalping settlers
'Scalping' is cutting the skin and hair off a human skull, dead or alive. But who first came up with this charming idea?
a) The Indians.
b) The Dutch.
c) The British.

Answer: b) The Dutch decided the safest way to get rid of Indians wasn't in a battle – after all, you might lose! No, it was to take the Indians one at a time whenever you had the chance. Anyone who killed an Indian was rewarded with £12 in 1703 – rising to £100 in 1722. To prove you'd killed an Indian you had to take his scalp.

In the French and Indian War of 1756–63 the Brits picked up the charming scalp idea. They offered £5 for anyone who brought in a French scalp – but £100 if it was from the head of a French Catholic missionary! Top prize was £200 for the Delaware Indian chief Shinngass.

Don't you wonder how they could tell where a scalp came from? I mean to say, what's to stop someone skinning an animal and claiming a reward?

Did you know…?
We think that germ warfare is a modern invention. But in 1758 the Brit general Jeffrey Amherst gave his Indian enemies a peace offering. He gave them blankets.

Where did he get the blankets? From the corpses in the British smallpox hospital. Nasty!

Witch way to go

The Indians weren't the only ones to suffer at the hands of the nasty New England Puritans … even their wives and daughters weren't safe.

It all started in Salem, Massachusetts, 1692, when three little girls aged nine, ten and twelve became the cause of death and trouble. When Betty, Abigail and Ann started acting strangely the doctor came up with the answer…

Who could they blame? Betty's dad was the minister – so you couldn't blame him! But the family had a black slave, Tituba, who had been teaching the girls how to tell fortunes. It would be easy to blame her!

Now the witch-hunting rules were simple:

Of course, everyone accused had to accuse someone else to save their life and so it went on. A hundred and fifty people were accused of being witches – even though they knew they weren't!

They said daft things like…

Then Betty, Abigail and Ann said…

That should have put a stop to it. But the accusers said…

So 19 women were hanged. But the worst fate was saved for one of the men. He refused to say if he was guilty or not guilty. His punishment was to have stones piled on top of him till he suffocated and was crushed to death.

All because three little liars had some 'sport'.

Slave suffering

In 1619 the first African slaves came to the English colonies in Virginia. Not all the slaves survived the horrible journey...

- These people were kidnapped from the west coast of Africa, tied to other captives by their hands and necks and marched along the coast to the African ports. Many died on this journey.

- They were packed on to ships with just half a metre for each captive. They were packed like books on a library shelf. Some were allowed exercise on deck – many weren't. Many died on this journey too.

34

- If the suffocating air below decks didn't kill them then disease often did. Their only 'toilet' was an open bucket, shared by 100 people. A doctor looked in a diseased ship and reported...

The floor of their rooms was so covered with blood and mucus that it looked like a slaughterhouse.

- Dead slaves were simply thrown overboard. Those who lived were so weak that a quarter of them died in their first year in America.

WELCOME TO AMERICA, THE LAND OF THE FREE!

(America was called 'land of the free' in the song 'The Star Spangled Banner', written in 1814, 200 years after the first slaves landed in Virginia. Even in 1814 'land of the free' was still a joke! It became the USA National Anthem in 1931.)

From the 1660s states started to make laws to control their slaves. They said…

Plotting against white owners will be punished by death.

Telling lies in court will be punished by...
1 Having an ear nailed to a post.
2 Being whipped.
3 Having the nailed ear cut off.

Meetings of four slaves or more are banned – even for funerals.

Striking a white person a second time will be punished by having the nose slit and the face burned.

Guess what the punishment was for a white person who **killed** a slave?

That's right – the white person would *not* be punished **unless** it was deliberate murder … and then they got just **three** months in jail.

ROTTEN REVOLUTIONARIES

In the mid 1700s the people of America were ruled by the Brits. Laws were passed in Britain's House of Commons and taxes were paid to Britain.

The Americans said...

And so it began.

Rotten revolutionaries timeline

1763 French and Indian War ends. Brits have paid for the defence of their American citizens and expect Americans to pay taxes to help with the cost. Brits ask for a 'Sugar Tax' to keep them sweet. Americans very cross and rebellious. Watch out Britain…

1765 An American mob destroys the Brit governor's house in Boston. Brits send in troops to boss Boston … and pinch the jobs of the Boston men! This spells t-r-o-u-b-l-e!

1770 Brit 'peace-keeping' soldiers in Boston are stoned by a mob. They fire on the mob and five Americans are killed. The Americans call it 'The Boston Massacre'. A couple of soldiers are found guilty of manslaughter and are branded on the thumb. But the Americans want real revenge.

1773 Boston rebels dress up as Indians and dump British tea in the harbour as a protest against a tea tax. It makes the tea taste awful and upsets the Brits.

1774 America creates its own parliament – called 'The Continental Congress' (which sounds posher). Meanwhile the Americans start to arm themselves.

1775 Brit Redcoat soldiers march into the countryside to disarm the

Americans. Fights break out at Lexington and Concord. Battle of Bunker Hill leaves rebels beaten but not crushed. They'll be back. Americans choose George Washington to lead their rebel armies.

1776 2 July. As the Brit armies struggle to defeat them, Americans make their 'Declaration of Independence'. But the President signs it on 4 July so that's when Americans have parties. (The 'Declaration of Independence' begins: 'All men are created equal'. What they really meant was 'All men are created equal – unless they happen to be Indian, black or female'!)

1783 Treaty of Paris makes peace. The Americans are free from British rule and...

1789 ...George Washington is elected President of the 13 American states – the United States of America. But those bashing Brits will be back!

Dying for America

The trouble with newspapers is they tell their readers what they want to hear – so they sell more newspapers! Reports get a bit twisted. Take the little bit of trouble in Boston in 1770. You might call it a 'disturbance' or a bit of 'unrest'. But to the angry Americans it was something else...

6 March 1770

ꮞ The Boston News ꮞ

MASSACRE

Brutal Brits slaughter Boston crowd

Last night a peaceful protest by Boston people turned to cruel carnage when rampant Redcoats turned their guns on our suffering citizens.

Redcoats have not only been bullying our city for two years, but they have also been taking our jobs. Our men are short of work yet these British bandits have been working in our docks to make extra money in their spare time. All our gentle waterfront workers wanted to do was march to show how upset they are.

The workers were faced by nine heavily armed Redcoats who blocked their way. The workers threw a few insults – 'Kill the Redcoat swine!' and little jesting comments like that. These were followed by a few snowballs. There may have been ice or stones in the snowballs but that was probably by accident.

Then the fatal word rang out across the street. And the word was 'Fire!' (It has been reported that a Boston trouble-maker shouted 'Fire' in order to start a real riot, but we don't believe that, do we?)

No sooner was the word shouted than a musket shot smashed into 54-year-old sailor Crispus Attucks and he fell dead on the spot.

Not satisfied with staining our lovely streets with innocent blood, the vicious Brits went on to gun down another four of Boston's sons!

The next blood to be shed will be British because this Boston Massacre must mean the start of a revolt against our cruel masters!

The Boston Five shall not die in vain!

Of course, five victims are terrible... but not really a massacre.

Still, it gave the American leaders an excuse to stir up trouble against the Brits. They didn't want the Brits to rule kindly – they wanted the Brits out altogether.

The truth? The rioters asked for it – actually *asked* for it! They gathered round the Redcoats and shouted in their face:

In the end, they fired.

Tea-hee!

B-o-s-t-o-n spelled Trouble for the Brits with a capital 'Tea', and after the massacre-that-wasn't came the 'Tea party-that-wasn't' in 1773.

The Brits said…

WE WILL SEND YOU CHEAP TEA FROM OUR EAST INDIA COMPANY. YOU CAN'T BUY YOUR TEA FROM ANYWHERE ELSE AND THERE WILL BE A SMALL TAX ON IT. BUT IT WILL STILL BE A REAL BARGAIN

And the ungrateful Americans said, 'No thanks!'

When the Brits tried to ship it to America anyway the Americans set off to tip it from the ships into the harbour at Boston.

The rebels dressed as Mohawk Indians and had this jolly song…

RALLY, MOHAWKS, BRING OUT YOUR AXES, AND TELL KING GEORGE WE'LL PAY NO TAXES ON HIS FOREIGN TEA.
HIS THREATS ARE WEAK, HE'S MAD TO THINK HE'LL FORCE OUR GIRLS AND WIVES TO DRINK HIS FILTHY TEA!

They jumped on the ship and were careful not to damage it or steal any tea. The main victim was the captain of the tea ship. They took all his clothes off, gave him a beating and covered him in mud.

And he was LUCKY! Because the usual rebel way of treating enemies was to cover them in tar and stick feathers into the tar. Mud washes off but tar often takes your skin and hair off with it! There was going to be a lot of tar and feathers flying once this 'tea party' led to all-out revolution.

Slave power

In 1775 the Brits offered a deal to the American slaves...

The slaves who slipped away to join Lord Dunmore's Brit army were trained and went into battle with white sashes across their chest – the sashes were printed with the words 'Liberty to Slaves'.

The good news was a thousand slaves joined Dunmore ... but what was the bad news? Choose one of these three answers...

a) Their beautiful flashing white sashes made them a good target for the enemy muskets, of course! The 1,000 were all killed in battle.

b) When they were defeated in battle the 1,000 were sent back to their owners in chains.

c) Lord Dunmore broke his promise and didn't set free the survivors.

NEVER TRUST A LORD

Answer: c) You might be shocked to hear Lord Dunmore could break his promise! After all he was a British lord! But he did. He loaded the thousand brave slaves on to a ship, sailed to the West Indies and sold them to the sugar plantations. Then Lord Dunmore put the cash in his pocket and sailed home to Britain. So the lesson is...

Revolting women

The American Revolution wasn't just American men fighting against British men. The women played their parts too – fighting, spying and spitting!

Dangerous Debbie
Many women (and even children) followed their men on the trail to war. They washed, cooked and helped nurse the wounded. But Deborah Sampson dressed as a man and went into battle as one. She was wounded twice. The first time she was shot in the knee and faced an unusual problem...

And she limped off and let it heal itself. But her second wound was in the shoulder and she faced an even stranger problem. The army doctor, Dr Birney, discovered she was a woman but kept her secret and had her moved to his own home to rest. She was nursed by the doctor's niece, but...

After the war she made a good living going around the United States giving talks and telling her story.

Mad Molly

Molly Hays followed her husband into battle to keep him supplied with water. She carried it to him in a pitcher so she got the nickname, 'Molly Pitcher'. But Molly Pitcher was no picture of loveliness. She smoked, chewed and spat tobacco, and she swore like a soldier.

> HORRIBLE HISTORIES HEALTH WARNING:
> Don't try being a Molly Pitcher at home. Especially don't try smoking, chewing, spitting and swearing all at the same time or you will probably choke.

Her husband's job was to clean the inside of a cannon barrel after it had been fired. At the Battle of Monmouth Court House she was just bringing him his water when he was shot dead.

Did Molly cry? Did she run away? Nah! She just picked up his cleaning 'rammer' and took his place at the cannon!

A story told by a soldier at Monmouth is too rude to repeat in a children's history book. But this is a *Horrible Histories* book, so here goes! Joseph Martin said...

> *Molly was reaching for a cartridge so her legs were stretched as wide as possible. Just then an enemy cannon shot past between her legs. The only damage was that it ripped off her skirts. She looked at the damage, not worried, and said, 'Just as well it didn't go a bit higher! It would have taken away something else!'*

Lydia's lugholes

In 1777 British General Howe marched into Philadelphia and told American woman Lydia Darragh he wanted to use her house as a meeting place.

Now you or I would have said, 'Push off you bat-faced, bean-brained, bullying Brit!' But what would have happened if she'd done that? The soldiers would have thrown her out anyway.

Lydia was cleverer than that. She said, 'You're welcome – I'm not interested in the war. But can I live upstairs while you use the rooms downstairs for your meetings?'

General Howe fell for it and let her stay. His first mistake.

His second mistake was to have no guard at the door to his meeting room. Lydia just sneaked downstairs and put her ear to the door. She heard the British plan to attack the Americans!

Next day she walked five miles to pass on the secret to George Washington's rebel army.

Washington was ready for Howe's attack, beat back the British and saved his army to fight another day ... and win in the end.

Bad Ben

Benedict Arnold is famous in American history as a traitor. He switched sides to give American secrets to the British enemy. He then fought for his new Brit friends.

Benedict had been wounded at Quebec and Saratoga in the same leg while he had been fighting for America against the Brits. Rebel leader Thomas Jefferson was desperate to get his hands on Bad Benedict to get some revenge. He said...

If we catch him we'll cut off that American leg and bury it with honour ... the rest of him we'll hang!

They never did catch him and Bad Ben moved to England. He was never very popular with anyone, not even the Brits, and died in debt. Thomas Jefferson must have been glad of that...

SEE! CHEATS NEVER BEATS

Georgie Porgie pudding and ... lie

George Washington was made commander of the American forces to fight the Brits. He also went on to become the first President of the new United States of America. He is remembered as an HONEST man. But was he?

When it came to fighting, Honest Georgie lost a lot of battles until he learned how to cheat a bit! Here's how to do it...

Chestnut Ridge

28 May 1754. George started his army career fighting for the British against the French. His partner, an Indian chief, wanted to attack a small French army camp at Chestnut Ridge. George did this BUT...

Cheat 1 There was a truce between the French and the British at the time! (This is a bit like you saying, 'Let's be friends!' to the smallest kid in class ... and, as he reaches out to shake hands, you punch him on the nose!)

Cheat 2 George attacked before dawn, in heavy rain so the French couldn't see him coming till the last moment. (This is a bit like taking the light bulb out of your sister's bedroom before you sneak in and pour a bucket of water over her!)

Cheat 3 When Georgie's troops attacked the front of the fort the French tried to run out of the back – wouldn't you? But George's Indian friends were waiting there to flatten the French. When Frenchman Joseph Coulon walked towards Georgie to surrender, the Indian chief smashed Coulon's skull with a club. (That's a bit like waiting till the final whistle in a soccer match – then tackling your opponent and breaking his leg!)

Ten Frenchmen were killed and one escaped – the one who escaped had left the camp to have an early morning piddle!

The Delaware crossing

26 December 1776. Georgie Washington was fighting against the British forces now. But he still used his favourite trick. He led 2,400 Americans across the

Delaware River to attack Hessian troops (from Germany), who were fighting for Britain. But…

Cheat 1 He did it at night again! This man must have been a very bad sleeper. He preferred battle at night to bed at night.

Cheat 2 He attacked the day after Christmas when all the Hessian troops were drunk. Christmas! The time of peace and goodwill and joy! When those poor Hessians could expect a bit of a lie-in! (This is like you choosing Christmas to drop stink-bombs through the letterbox of your nasty neighbour. You just *wouldn't* choose that day, would you?)

Cheat 3 His men attacked the Hessians in their beds. They didn't just jump on them and say, 'Happy Christmas – you're a prisoner!' No! They said, 'Happy Christmas – you're dead!' and killed a hundred.

Was Georgie a fair fighter? Does Father Christmas have a purple beard? No! No! No!

Hessian horrors

One-third of Georgie's British army enemies came from Hesse in Germany and were scary and fierce for Americans to face. These Hessians were being paid to fight for Britain. So George Washington and his government came up with…

Cheat 1 They paid the Hessian soldiers NOT to fight them! Georgie was 'armed' with bits of paper. The papers had promises of free land to any Hessian soldier who switched sides. (This is a bit like bribing the other team's best players to leave the pitch as soon as you start the match! Not much of a game!)

Cheat 2 Of course the real cheat was that the land the Americans promised didn't belong to them at all. It was the land of the Indians. The Hessians had the problem of taking the land...

In the end Georgie Washington and the Americans won the War of Independence not because they had the greatest general – but because the British army were even worse than the American forces and were fighting a long way away from home.

George was rewarded six years later by being made President – and the British Colony of America became 'The United States of America', all the way from the Atlantic to the Mississippi ... though, as usual, nobody asked the Indians.

Foul firsts

1 First baddie

Possibly the first US baddie was London ruffian John Billington who landed at Plymouth Rock from the *Mayflower* in 1620. During the trip, to stop him swearing and

51

upsetting the godly Pilgrims, Captain Standish tied Billington's feet to his neck!

In 1630, he was hanged for shooting a fellow-Pilgrim – the first (but certainly not the last) recorded execution in American history.

2 First vigilantes

In the 1760s murderers and thieves were roaming the backwoods of South Carolina and there were no sheriffs to stop them. So some locals called themselves 'regulators' – meaning vigilantes – to put a stop to these crude criminal capers. What would you do if you caught a killer? There was no jail and who would guard the killer and who would pay to feed him till his trial? Answer: Never mind a trial! Execute him! Much easier. Not all captured outlaws were handed over to the law. Many were killed on the spot, usually by being flogged to death and sometimes to the rhythm of fiddles.

3 First gang

In 1770s, the Doane Gang was America's first outlaw gang of brothers. The brothers (led by Moses) plus 12 pals, fought for King George in Pennsylvania. How did they serve their king? By stealing whatever they could find from the Americans with the help of muskets, knives and tomahawks. After the defeat of King George's British army, they continued to raid farms and villages. Eventually, most were caught and hanged. The nickname for thieving rogues was 'Tories'.

4 First stagecoach highwayman

Joseph T Hare was born in Pennsylvania. He started out in the New Orleans area, stealing purses from lone travellers. After a spell in prison, he went north. In 1818 he held up the Baltimore night coach and stole $15,000. Two days later he was arrested buying an expensive coat in a posh shop, and he was hanged in September 1818. He may have been the first, but he didn't last very long.

5 First river pirates

At the time of the Doane gang Sam Mason was a loyal American outlaw. He stole from the British! When the War of Independence was over he kept up the wicked work though, raiding riverboats on the Mississippi and other rivers. His favourite trick was to get himself hired as a pilot to guide a boat through difficult water. He would then run the boat aground near to where his gang was hidden.

Sometimes, he had help from a wicked woman who'd call out to a passing boat from an island. 'Help me! I'm stranded!' she'd cry. As soon as the boat came near, other gang members used fast canoes to attack. Governors of Louisiana and Mississippi put a price on his head.

6 First bounty hunter

Where there's a reward there's usually someone out to collect it – a 'bounty hunter'. In the 1770s bounty hunter Bill Sitter captured river pirate Sam Mason and delivered his head – one report says in a bottle, another in a ball of clay!

But Bill Sitter was then recognized from a scar on his chest – he wasn't Bill Sitter at all! He was Wiley Harp, a well-known killer. He was then hanged – and he never got to collect his bounty!

THE NASTY NINETEENTH CENTURY

The new United States of America finally got rid of the bossy Brits. Then it was time to get rid of those Indians who had the cheek to have lived there for 10,000 years. History was about to become really horrible – especially for the Indians...

Nasty nineteenth century timeline

1812 Brits at war with USA's old friend France. Brits say they can capture US ships or sailors to help in the war effort. USA says, 'No you can't! We'll fight you!' War again. Brits attack Canada from the north and their Indian friends, led by Tecumseh, attack Americans from the west. Peace in 1814 with Brits and Indians beaten back.

1831 Indians are getting in the way of settlers moving west. So the Indians are told to move even further west. At this rate they'll be in the Pacific Ocean – or dead. Guess which?

1846 Americans give the Indians a break and attack the Mexicans instead. 'One of the most unjust wars ever waged against a weak nation!' Who said that? US General Ulysses Grant! The USA wins half a million square miles of new land.

1848 Gold discovered in California which has just been won from Mexico! Lucky USA. In the next few years they'll get $200 million worth of gold from California.

1861 The Civil War starts between the Northern and the Southern states.
1864 Black Kettle's Indians in Colorado make peace – and their reward is to be massacred at Sand Creek.
1866 The Civil War is over so the Americans can give more time to moving west and driving Indians from the land. Sioux Indian chief Red Cloud fights back.
1868 General Custer sets out with the 7th Cavalry to destroy unfriendly Indians wherever he can find them.
1874 The northern Indians had been safe in their Black Hills of Dakota. Now gold is discovered there. It won't be long before American miners move in.
1876 The Indians rebel against the invading miners and General Custer goes in to sort out Chief Crazy Horse, Chief Sitting Bull and their Sioux troublemakers. But it is Custer who is killed.
1877 The mighty American army turns its full force on the Indians. Crazy Horse is penned in his reservation and Sitting Bull flees to Canada. It's the end for the free Native American Indians.
1890 Battle of Wounded Knee, on the Oglala Sioux Reservation, South Dakota. The Indians had surrendered but were surrounded and 153 killed – including women and babies.

The Removals

Once the settlers started to move west they met the Indians who lived there. The Indians weren't too keen to share their lands with the new settlers and fighting broke out.

President Jackson, Indian-killer, came up with an answer: 'Removal'. Old 'Long Knife', as the Indians called Jackson, said…

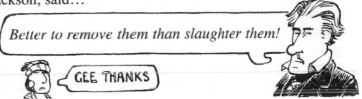

Better to remove them than slaughter them!

GEE THANKS

'Removal' sounded a nicer thing than 'chuck them across the river into the wilds'. So from 1831 they were 'removed' west of the Mississippi.

- The ones who didn't want to go were massacred.
- The ones who did go died of pneumonia in the winter and cholera in the summer.
- A quarter of the Cherokees who were moved died before they even got to their new 'home' in the west. The journey killed them.

The Indians never called this the 'Removal' – they called it 'The Trail of Tears'.

Forget the western films of cowboys and Indians fighting on the plains in the 1880s. The Indian nations were really destroyed back in 1830s by Old Long Knife.

Sand Creek and scalps

The American settlers began to spread into Indian lands. These white invaders began to wipe out the buffalo that the Indians needed to survive.

The Indians tried to stop them and they could be very cruel too. In particular they liked to use the trick they learned from their white attackers. Scalping.

A US soldier described what he found in an Indian camp after they'd destroyed it...

> *I saw some of our men opening bundles. I watched them take out a number of white person's scalps – men's, women's and children's. I saw the scalp of one woman in particular. It had been taken entirely off the head – the head had been skinned, taking all the hair, and then tanned to stop it rotting. The hair was reddish-brown and hung in ringlets. It was very long hair. There were two holes in the front of the scalp so the Indians could tie it on their head when they appeared in the scalp dance.*

A traveller came across another Indian massacre and wrote...

> *About a hundred yards from a deserted ranch we came across the body of a murdered woman and her two dead children. One child was a little girl of four years and the other even younger. The woman had been stabbed in several places and scalped. The two children had had their throats cut, their heads being nearly separated from their bodies.*

When the American army heard these stories they thought it would be fair to take their revenge. In 1864 at Sand Creek, Colorado, they went on the attack.

If you were the commander, Colonel John Chivington, who would you attack?

a) A tribe of 600 men, women and children that had made peace and settled in a village for the winter.

b) A tribe of 600 warriors who were camped in the hills and raiding cattle ranches.

Answer: a) Of course they picked on the Indians who had made peace.

The people of Colorado were annoyed that the Cheyenne and Arapaho group had made peace before they could be caught and killed. So Chivington decided to kill them anyway, and headed for the Indians' winter camp at Sand Creek.

Chivington cried...

> *Remember the murdered women and children!*

... and led the charge.

How did the soldiers 'remember the murdered women and children'? By murdering women and children, of course!

Some soldiers were shocked by the massacre. One wrote…

> *The women and children were scalped and their brains knocked out. Our men used their knives to rip open the women and club the little children; they knocked them in the head with their guns and beat their brains out. They damaged the bodies in any way they could.*

Another said…

> *There was one little child, probably three years old, just big enough to walk through the sand. His family had gone ahead and this little fellow was following behind.*

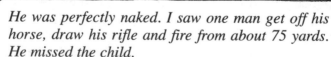

> *He was perfectly naked. I saw one man get off his horse, draw his rifle and fire from about 75 yards. He missed the child.*

A glorious victory? Every dead man, woman and child was scalped and horribly carved up by the soldiers' knives.

Yet Colonel Chivington proudly declared...

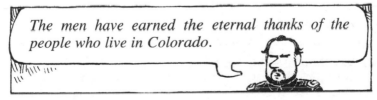

Horror followed horror. It's called 'revenge'. Make up your own mind who is most to blame.

How horrible are you?

Could you have lived 130–150 years ago on the American plains? Here are some true events. What would you have done if you'd been there?

1 You're in a battle when a friend slaps you on the shoulder. He points to his mouth. An arrow has hit him and is fastened in his tongue. What will you do to help him?
a) Give him an aspirin to kill the pain.
b) Take him 50 miles, in agony, to the nearest doctor.
c) Cut his tongue out.

2 You have carried out a massacre but want to leave a clear message for your enemies. How do you do this?
a) Leave them a note saying, 'If you don't leave us alone this will happen to you!'
b) Deliver the bodies to your enemy's camp and say 'That's what happens if you mess with us!'
c) Cut out the eyes of the victims and lay them on the rocks around the battlefield.

3 You have shot and stabbed an enemy. Just when you think he is dead and begin to scalp him ... he jumps up and begs for mercy. What do you do?
a) Say 'Sorry' and try to stick his scalp back on.
b) Set him free as he will probably die from his wounds anyway.
c) Shoot him in the head so you can finish the scalping job in peace.

4 You are an Indian woman in a village under attack by soldiers. What can you do to help?
a) Hide in a tent and keep the children happy with a game of I-spy.
b) Stand behind your warrior husband and keep him supplied with arrows.
c) Grab a weapon and scalp every soldier you can kill.

5 You are an army commander and your camp is under attack. What can you do to save your women and children from being taken prisoner and tortured?
a) Give up without a fight so your enemy will be kind to the women and children.
b) Put the women and children in the safest part of the camp so they can't be captured till every defender has been killed.
c) Put them in your gunpowder store. If you are losing the battle then set off the gunpowder and blow your wives and children to tiny pieces.

6 A friend is bitten on the finger by a rattlesnake. He will die if the poison gets to the rest of his body. What do you do to help him?
a) Wrap a bandage round the finger.
b) Suck out the poison.
c) Chop off his finger.

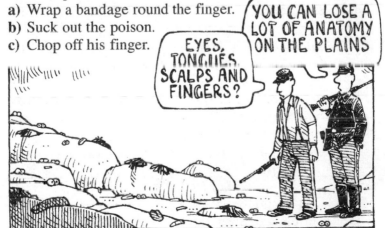

63

Answers: All **a)** answers score 1, all **b)** score 2 and all **c)** score 3. Add up your total.

6–10 You are probably too gentle for the Indian wars. Stay in the 21st Century and don't touch anything sharper than your knitting needles.

11–15 You are a bit of a bully, aren't you? The local nursery school kids probably run and hide when you walk down the street! But you wouldn't last long in the days of the Indian wars.

16–18 Wow! I hope I don't bump into you on some dark night! You are as hard as a school-dinner pea and nearly as dangerous.

The truth? All the **c)** answers actually happened. Here's how…

1 Captain Henry Palmer described how he helped a soldier in 1865…

> *The point of an arrow had passed through his open mouth and stuck in the root of his tongue. As we had no doctor with us, it was decided that to get the arrow out from his mouth the tongue must be, and was, cut out.*

Which is a lesson for us all! If you ever get into a battle, keep your big mouth shut!

2 At the Fetterman massacre in 1866 a troop of soldiers were tricked into a trap and massacred. The victims had been hacked to pieces, eyes left on rocks along with brains and guts. Only one soldier's body was untouched. It was the body of the young bugle player, Adolph Metzler. A soldier explained...

> *The bravery of our bugler was well-known. He had killed several Indians by beating them over the head with his bugle. He fought so bravely the Indians honoured him by leaving his remains untouched but covered by a buffalo robe.*

BRAVE BUGLE BOY BUFFALO BLANKET

Of course if he'd used a gun instead of a bugle he may have lived! Don't try this with a school orchestra trumpet – you'll dent it terribly.

3 Lieutenant William Drew described how a 'dead' Indian came back to life to plead for his scalp. Drew said...

> *The Indians believe that if a warrior loses his scalp he cannot go to His Happy Hunting Ground (Heaven) when he dies. Indians will lose their lives and show no fear, but they will try to save their scalps.*

Remember that next time you have a haircut! If you are knocked over by a bus as you walk home from the barber's shop you won't get to Heaven!

4 Captain Henry Palmer said his troop of soldiers were ordered to spare the women and children – but kill every Indian male over the age of 12. Wasn't that sweet of the caring captain? Anyway, he said they had a problem when they tried *not* to kill the women…

> *Sadly for the women and children our men hadn't time to aim carefully. Bullets and arrows from both sides filled the air. Squaws and children, as well as warriors, fell among the dead and wounded. Many of the female members of the tribe fought as bravely as their savage husbands.*

Those of you who have seen a schoolgirls' hockey match will believe this very easily.

5 In 1866 an officer wrote…

> *The colonel gave orders that the women and children should be held in the gunpowder store. If all was lost he himself would blow up the store and take the lives of all, rather than let the Indians capture any of them alive.*

DADDY SAYS IF THE INDIANS COME WE'RE ALL GOING TO A PLACE CALLED SMITHEREENS

6 Will Comstock was an Indian fighter. An American magazine once reported…

Comstock is known to the Indians as 'Medicine Bill'. The reason for this, Comstock says, is because he cut off a man's finger after it had been bitten by a rattlesnake. This saved the man's life and earned him a great amount of respect from the Arapaho Indians.

Imagine going to Medicine Bill's house for tea and biscuits! What would you do if he offered you chocolate-covered fingers?

Prairie poetry

Custer set out to win fame and fortune by killing Indians. The army *said* he was there to control them – but if the Indians gave trouble he 'controlled' them by killing them. Custer, with his long blond hair, looked a real hero. Pity the brains were a bit short under the blond scalp!

In 1876 Custer led his men on a death-or-glory attack on Sioux Indians camped at the Little Big Horn River. It was madness. They got the death – but now they can have the glory in a poem!

The interesting thing is the Indians were desperate to get their tomahawks on General George Custer's famous long, blond scalp. But he had his hair cut before he set off. So, while many of his soldiers were scalped after the massacre, Custer wasn't. The haircut confused the Indians, who didn't recognize him!

General Custer's haircut

General Custer went for a ride
By the Big Horn River side.
He took his guns, he took his men,
But none of them came back again
(At least not alive).

General Custer's scouts had a spy,
And said, 'The Sioux are quite close by!'
Custer said, 'I'll shoot them every one...
But not till I've had my hair done!'
(Short back and sides.)

General Custer said, 'I'm a winner!
We'll be back in time for dinner!'
But when they reached the Sioux tepees,
There were braves as far as the eye could see!
(Oooops!)

So Custer fought and his army died,
By the Big Horn River side.
But Custer's skin stayed on his head,
His haircut saved his scalp, they said...
(... but not his life).

Did you know…?

General Custer was famous for more than his hair! He was famous for his bum! Custer was such a tough, long-distance rider the Indians called him 'Hard Backside'!

Fatally Wounded Knee

After Custer's defeat at the Little Big Horn the army became even more cruel. Crazy Horse was captured and killed just a year after Custer's death.

Chief Sitting Bull's desperate Indians had a strange belief that if they performed their 'Ghost Dance', and wore magical 'Ghost Shirts', then the army bullets couldn't hurt them.

In 1890 Chief Sitting Bull returned from hiding in Canada. He was captured, but during his arrest he was killed. (Maybe he wasn't wearing his Ghost Shirt?)

Later that December Chief Big Foot decided to surrender to the army and, with his tribe, they took him to a place called 'Wounded Knee'. What happened next was the last great massacre of the Indians.

No one is quite sure how it happened but it seems to be this…

The Indians were never a great force again.

Did you know…?

On 28 February 1973, members of the American Indian Movement seized the village of Wounded Knee and invited the government to repeat the massacre. They argued for 72 days, but finally surrendered. They got a lot of publicity for the Sioux Indian problems. Two of their people were killed and many more wounded in fighting against law officers.

Golden greed

The greatest gold rush in the history of the United States began with the discovery of gold at Sutter's Mill on the American River in northern California on 24 January 1848.

When word reached San Francisco, thousands from that city and other parts of California flocked to the region. The people who arrived were called 'forty-niners' because it was 1848. (Well, it took them a long time to get there because cars and planes hadn't been invented!) California's population grew from about 14,000 in 1848 to 100,000 in 1850.

During the Californian Gold Rush, prospectors could get there in three main ways...

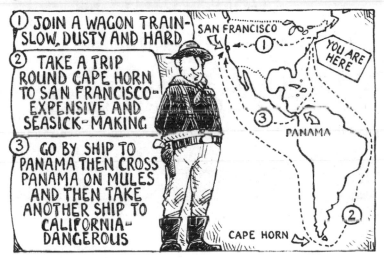

① JOIN A WAGON TRAIN- SLOW, DUSTY AND HARD

② TAKE A TRIP ROUND CAPE HORN TO SAN FRANCISCO- EXPENSIVE AND SEASICK-MAKING

③ GO BY SHIP TO PANAMA THEN CROSS PANAMA ON MULES AND THEN TAKE ANOTHER SHIP TO CALIFORNIA- DANGEROUS

SAN FRANCISCO
YOU ARE HERE
PANAMA
CAPE HORN

The problem with **3** was that Panama bandits robbed the prospectors on their way to the gold rush. (Yes, you're right, it would have made more sense to rob them on their way *back* when they had found gold – but the bandits weren't as bright as you.)

Then a businessman hired a Texas gunman – Randy Runnels – who set up a bandit-bashing bunch of bad-boys:

the 'Vigilantes of New Grenada'. This gang caught 78 Panama bandits and hanged them. They left the corpses dangling by the trail as a warning to others.

Terror towns

It wasn't just the journey to California that was dangerous. When you got there you could be robbed of your equipment or killed for your plot of land. Sheriffs and marshals were scarce, so miners took the law into their own hands.

There was one place that was especially keen to string up lawbreakers. What charming name was it given?

…of course. One of several strange place names. Like…

…a small town in the Sierra foothills. Sounds a bit dangerous.

…could be fun, but you wouldn't want to end up in…

If you did then it was time to head off to…

Name that place

America has a lot of peculiar place names. Here are ten. Can you spot the one that is NOT the name of a place?

1 Pee Pee (Ohio)
2 Looneyville (Texas)
3 Peculiar (Missouri)
4 Eek (Alaska)
5 Greasy Corner (Arkansas)
6 Dog's Breath (California)
7 Bowlegs (Oklahoma)
8 Bug (Kentucky)
9 Who'd A Thought It (Alabama)
10 Shittim Gulch (Washington)

Answer: Number 6 is the only invented one. The rest all exist!

Can you imagine saying...

The teacher may well tell you...

Awful for animals

In the history of the USA it was usually the innocent who suffered most. Women, children ... and animals. Here are a few tragic tails ... I mean tales...

1 Plucked pigeons When the Pilgrims landed in 1620 there must have been about nine BILLION birds known as passenger pigeons. One early settler said he saw a flock one mile wide and 240 miles long. (Think of all that bird poo falling like rain!) A 1770 report said there were so many birds that a hunter brought down 125 with a single shot from a blunderbuss.

They were slaughtered and used for pies or pig-food till they were almost gone by 1900. On 1 September 1914 the last one fell off its perch in Cincinnati Zoo.

2 Battered buffalo In 1830 there were 70 million buffalo rambling round the American plains. Sixty-five years later there were 800, and many of them were in zoos. Of course, many Indian tribes lived on buffalo – by exterminating the buffalo the Americans exterminated the Indians, without being seen to kill them. Very clever, and it worked. As the buffalo numbers fell, so did the Indian population – from two million to 90,000. Fewer Indians meant they needed less land, so the USA took another 86 million acres from them between 1887 and 1934. The USA made 400 treaties with Indians over the years and broke every single one. Like the old buffalo joke, it just isn't funny...

3 Scorched sheep Cattle ranchers and their cowboys accused 'woollies' of muddying waterholes so their cattle could not drink. They began a 'war' to drive out sheep farmers. In this war, sheep were dynamited, set fire to, and driven into rivers. Others were shot, knifed, poisoned with saltpetre (deadly to sheep but not to cattle) or 'rimrocked' (driven over a cliff).

In the end, they realized that sheep could graze on land unfit for cattle and that ranchers could keep both sheep and cattle! The wars ended.

4 Massacred mules In the 1880s the US Army used mules to carry their supplies into the Indian wars. Of course the mules were shot at by the Indians and killed. The soldiers would often say, 'Thanks very much,' and eat the mule! A mule corpse was also a good thing to hide behind and rest your rifle on. If the attack went on for a few days, as it did at the Battle of Arickaree in 1868, then the mule meat went mouldy and maggoty. John Hurst was an army scout at

75

Arickaree and described the delight of eating mule meat...

> We had nothing to eat but dead horses and mules which were rotting all around us. When we cut into this meat the stench was something frightful and it had green streaks running through it. The only way we could make it fit for eating was by sprinkling gunpowder over it while it was cooking which took away some of the foul smell.

OOPS... TOO MUCH GUNPOWDER

Next time your mother offers you cheap sausages for tea sprinkle gunpowder over them! They may not taste any better but at least you can enjoy some real bangers!

5 Hunlucky horses In 1862, two Rebel regiments from Mississippi and Georgia stumbled into each other in Virginia and opened fire. In the rain and confusion, the only victim was one horse. And it wasn't just in war that horses suffered. In the early 1900s, 15,000 horses a year died on the streets of New York, many worked to death. Sometimes they were left to rot for days when the owners walked off and left the horse corpses. That's probably where the unfunny joke came from...

I SAY, I SAY, I SAY, WHAT HAS FOUR LEGS, A TAIL AND FLIES?

A DEAD HORSE!

6 Dreadful for dogs The Indian villages on the Plains were usually full of dogs. They were useful as guard dogs, of course, but they were useful for something else. Dinner. A soldier visited a chief's tent and described the feast he was offered…

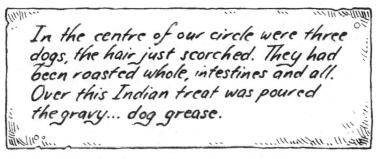

In the centre of our circle were three dogs, the hair just scorched. They had been roasted whole, intestines and all. Over this Indian treat was poured the gravy… dog grease.

Can you imagine coming home to tepee tea?

WHAT'S FOR TEA, MUM?

YOUR FAVOURITE - HOT DOGS!

7 Rotten for rattlers Rattlesnakes have a rattle at one end and a very nasty pair of fangs at the other. You wouldn't want to rile a rattler, would you? The Indians did! An American magazine described what they did to the woeful worm…

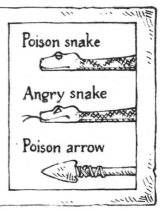

The rattlesnake is caught and caged. He is made angry by being poked with sticks. A piece of deer liver is held towards him on the end of a stick. Into this he strikes his poisoned fangs. An arrow head is dipped into the poison and the Indians have a poison-tipped arrow.

Poison snake

Angry snake

Poison arrow

One of those arrows in your bum would be a real pain in the backside! The only cure is to get a friend to suck out the poison!

8 Suffering strays In the 1860s the inventor Thomas Edison was trying to sell his 'direct current' electrical systems. His great rival was George Westinghouse, who had an 'alternating current' system. Edison wanted to show people how dangerous alternating current could be. He paid children to gather stray dogs who then had electricity shot through them till they died. Poor pooches! His invention of the electric chair was just as cruel – the first victim, William Kemmler, was given 50 seconds of alternating current ... he cried out and smouldered a little but didn't die. It took a second bigger blast to kill him. Very messy, but it didn't stop many of the American states using the machines. In some states today men and women can still die in electric chairs ... but at least it's against the law to kill a dog in one!

9 Painful for ponies In the 1870s the US Army forced the Indians to live in special areas called 'reservations'. The Indians wanted to leave these reservations from time to time to hunt buffalo – especially as they often went hungry. The army came up with a great idea to stop the Indians from escaping. They slaughtered their ponies!

THE UNCIVIL WAR

In 1808 writer William Jenks says...

> *The northern states will fight the southern states and the fight will be about slavery... The northern states will defeat the exhausted southern states in a war that lasts four years... After the war we will have a new United States of America...*

All these things will come true 53 years *later* when Jenks is long dead. He gets one fact a little wrong...

> *This war will begin in 1856!*

The war actually began in 1861, but the violence started in ... guess when? Yes...

Uncivil war timeline

1856 The people of Missouri State want to keep slaves and they attack Kansas which can't make up its mind. The famous John Brown hated slavers. He hacked the Missouri attackers to pieces, saying he was backed by Almighty God.

1859 John Brown attacks US Army at Harper's Ferry in Virginia. Slaves don't rise to support him so he is

GO GET 'EM JOHNNY!

WE'VE GOT BACKING FOR OUR HACKING!

caught and hanged. His supporters say he died for his fellow men, just like Christ … but Christ didn't go around hacking his enemies to death!

1860 Abraham Lincoln is elected 16th President – he's going to ban slavery and the Rebels in the south won't like that!

1861 War starts when Rebels attack Fort Sumter, South Carolina.

1862 Desperate Rebels force men to join their army while President Lincoln says 'All slaves are free!' Black slaves run off to join Lincoln – but the whites don't want to fight with them.

1863 Rebels lose their best general, 'Stonewall' Jackson when he is accidentally shot by his own men! When the southern Rebels try to invade the north they are crushed at 'Gettysburg' and will not recover.

1864 7,000 men die in just 20 minutes of fighting at 'Cold Harbor'. General Sherman's northern forces start their devastating 'March to the Sea' to destroy the southern Rebels.

1865 The Rebels allow black slaves to fight with them but the ungrateful people jeer and spit at the black soldiers. The Rebels surrender in April but less than a week later President Lincoln is assassinated by an actor, John Wilkes Booth.

Yankee doodle and the rebels

The people of the north called themselves Billy Yank. (Hank Yank would have been more fun but the swanky Yankees were serious about their hanky panky.) Where did the word 'Yank' come from?

Well, the old British settlers had sneered at the Dutch settlers in New York. They thought these cheese-making Dutch people were a joke. They called any Dutchman 'John Cheese' and the Dutch for John Cheese is 'Jan Kees' – pronounced yan-kees!

The name stuck to northern Americans like Edam cheese sticks to your granny's false teeth. Northern Americans became Jan Kees or Yankees.

fig Ⅲ			
cheeses	yankees	yankee cheeses	cheesey yankees

The people of the south wanted to rebel against the Billy Yanks so they called themselves Johnny Rebels or Johnny Rebs for short (because it's easier to spell).

The northern Yanks and the southern Rebs had the usual conversation...

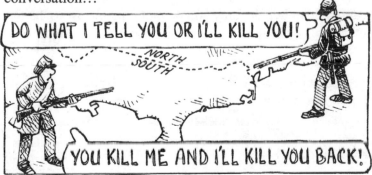

It meant war – the American Civil War.

Did you know...?

Abraham Lincoln was ready to go to war to abolish slavery in the southern states of the USA, but he was still a racist. He wanted *free* blacks but he didn't want *equal* blacks. He said...

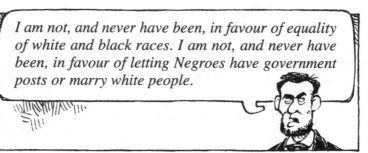

I am not, and never have been, in favour of equality of white and black races. I am not, and never have been, in favour of letting Negroes have government posts or marry white people.

That's nasty.

Rotten shots

Yanks and Rebs were rotten shots right from the first day of the war. The Rebs attacked Fort Sumter at Charleston and used cannon to wipe out the defenders. Reb Edmund Ruffin fired the first shot and 34 hours later they had fired 4,000 shells into the fort. How many Yankee defenders died? Not one! But the Yankees in the fort did surrender and 'saluted' the Rebs by firing 100 cannon. As they fired cannon number 50 they did something the Rebs hadn't managed with 4,000 – they killed one of their own defenders!

Round one to the Rebs.

In the end the Rebs lost the Civil War and that was more than Edmund Ruffin could stand. In June 1865 he shot himself in the head ... and, amazingly, he didn't miss!

It's amazing that over half a million people died in the Civil War because the soldiers were such rotten shots. Most couldn't hit a barn if they were standing inside it! General Ulysses S Grant complained...

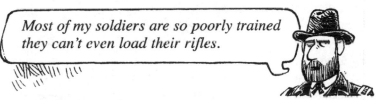

Most of my soldiers are so poorly trained they can't even load their rifles.

And that was true. After the Battle of Gettysburg there were 37,000 rifles abandoned on the field.

- 24,000 were still loaded
- 18,000 had at least two bullets in the barrel
- 6,000 had up to ten bullets jammed in
- 1 rifle had 24 bullets and powder loaded

(If the 24-bullet soldier had pulled the trigger he'd certainly have killed someone – himself! The rifle would have exploded.)

Fight like a Civil War soldier

To act out a Civil War battle is simple. Most of them were fought the same way.

You need:
Two armies – say the boys against the girls in your class.
Two generals, one on each side.
Weapons – water pistols are good and deadly.

To fight:
First choose your battle ground. (A playing field is better than the playground because it doesn't show the blood.)
The generals line up their army in a straight line.
The generals stay safe at the back and order their troops to march forward.
When the two lines are in range they stop and open fire.

Scoring:
The side that doesn't run away is the winner.

And that's about it. Even your teacher could have been a Civil War general!

Civil War quiz torture

Torment your teacher or pester your parent with these fiendishly fascinating but fairly foul questions:

1 Reb General Robert E Lee died on 12 October 1870 at Lexington, Virginia. He should have been buried in full uniform but they left his boots off. Why?
a) Because his feet had swelled and they couldn't get them back on the corpse.
b) Because the coffin was too small. It was a choice of leaving the boots off or slicing a bit off the top of his head.

c) Because his starving wife had cooked his boots to make a stew for the funeral guests.

2 Reb General Beauregard was famous for this thick black hair. It turned grey during the war. Why?
a) Because he ran out of hair dye.
b) Because the horrors of war turned his hair grey with shock.
c) Because he dyed it grey to escape capture.

3 Yank General McClellan was defeated by 'Quaker Guns'. What was so unusual about them?
a) They fired backwards so when you thought you were safe they shot you.
b) They made so much noise they made you quake till the buttons fell off your tunic and your trousers fell down.
c) They couldn't fire at all because they were made of wood.

4 Rebel General Thomas J Jackson, nicknamed 'Stonewall' Jackson, did something strange with his right forefinger. What?

a) He stood with it pointing up at the sky.

b) He lost it in a goat's mouth when he went to stroke the creature.

c) He bit his nails so hard he chewed the finger off.

5 The Rebs were short of gunpowder because it was all made in Yankee America. They found a way to make it using what?

a) Buffalo poo.

b) Frog guts.

c) Human piddle.

6 Two Reb brothers, Jasper and Jack Walker, each lost one in the Civil War. What?

a) A leg.

b) A mother.

c) A bet.

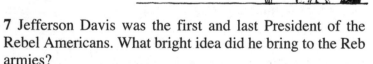

7 Jefferson Davis was the first and last President of the Rebel Americans. What bright idea did he bring to the Reb armies?

a) Reindeer to pull them through the snowy mountains.

b) Dolphins to pull their ships into battle when it was calm.

c) Camels to help them fight in the desert.

8 Yankee Benjamin Franklin Butler was given command of New Orleans and was hated by the defeated Rebs. They got their own back by putting his picture on what?
a) The front of dartboards for piercing.
b) The bottom of pots for piddling.
c) The middle of handkerchiefs for polluting.

9 Reb General Forrest hated black people. What was he said to do to black Yankee soldiers he captured?
a) Starve them to death.
b) Bury them alive.
c) Use them as slaves to serve his dinner.

10 Yankee troops captured Reb General Robert E Lee's tobacco plantation. They took out the tobacco and planted what?
a) Corpses.
b) General Lee's treasure so they could come back and find it after the war.
c) Explosive mines to kill the General if he ever returned.

Answers:
1b) A flood had washed away all the undertaker's coffins. Eventually one coffin was rescued downriver from the flood. It was too short for Lee's six-foot corpse, so he was buried without his boots. Quite a suitable end really – at the battle of Gettysburg, in 1863, many of Lee's poor soldiers died barefoot looking for shoes.
2a) Vain Beauregard didn't want to show his age so he dyed his hair with Yankee dye. But when the war came

he couldn't get the dye from the enemy and his hair turned back to its true grey colour.

3c) General McClellan had 100,000 men in his Yankee army. But his spies said the rebel enemy had 200,000 men. General McClellan decided not to attack. But the truth is the Rebs had only 15,000 men and a load of wooden Quaker (or dummy) cannon that fooled him. The Rebs often used this trick – and it always worked! It's a bit like a robber holding up a bank with a sawn-off cucumber!

4a) Many people think old Stonewall was mad – he refused to eat foods that he liked ... and if he started to like what he was eating he gave it up. He sucked lemons before going into battle and often stood with his right hand held up, index finger pointing skywards. He claimed...

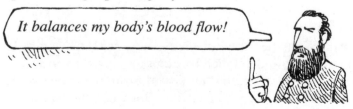

He was shy, had poor eyesight and was partly deaf. As a strict religious man he objected to fighting on Sundays. He was also the South's best general. In a series of battles in 1862 in Shenandoah Valley, he held off 80,000 Yankee troops with 15,000 men. On 1 May 1863, he was accidentally shot by his own soldiers. He was taken to a field hospital and his left arm was amputated two inches below the shoulder. He still had a right finger to point to the sky but it didn't help. He died of pneumonia on Sunday 10 May. His last words were...

I have always desired to die on a Sunday.

He was 39.

5c) At the start of the war George Washington Rains was given the job of setting up Reb gunpowder factories. But the Reb south had none of the main ingredient of gunpowder – potassium nitrate (saltpetre). George Rains ordered a hunt for saltpetre and some was eventually found in limestone caves, but it was not enough. George sent secret agents to Europe and 3,000,000 pounds were smuggled across the Atlantic. But this was still not enough, so George ordered his men to dig up old toilets and make saltpetre from the stale pee! George's gunpowder factories actually made a profit. After the war, Yankee soldiers captured George's gun-pee-owder factories and claimed that his powder was the finest they had ever used.

| Yankee gunpowder | Rebel gunpowder |
| POW! | PONG! |

6a) Jasper and Jack Walker from Charlotte, North Carolina, were Rebs. Jasper was wounded in the leg and captured at the Battle of Gettysburg. His leg was amputated and he was sent to a Yankee prison camp. Later in the war, brother Jack was also wounded and captured and had his leg amputated. After the war, the two one-legged brothers were a familiar sight in the town as they stumped about. On the day Jasper was to be married, he fell and broke his wooden leg. Not wanting to be married on one leg, he borrowed Jack's. It fitted perfectly and the wedding went ahead. Later the brothers often boasted how Jasper was the only man to get married while standing on somebody else's leg.

7c) Jefferson Davis worked with the Yankees until the war started. He made sure the Yankees had modern rifles – and that's what helped defeat the Rebs! Thanks, Jeff! His camel idea was just as disastrous. The main problem was that the tough Reb soldiers didn't want to ride side-saddle because it made them look like women!

8b) Butler was balding, fat and cross-eyed. Imagine that face staring up at you when you sat on a toilet pot! A Reb gambler called Mumford said, 'Butler is soft! If I chop down the Yankee flag I bet he doesn't dare do anything to me!' Mumford lost his bet when Butler had him hanged! Butler became known as 'Beast' Butler. Then Butler earned the nickname 'Spoons' when it was discovered that he had been stealing Rebel silver from rich-folks' homes. He was sent back to Washington.

9b) Nathan Bedford Forrest was a rich 40-year-old businessman and slave owner when he joined the Rebel Army. (He was not a very good horseman because he suffered from boils on his bottom.) In 1864, Major General Forrest sent 1,200 men to take Fort Pillow in Tennessee. This Yankee fort was held by 260 black and 295 white soldiers. The Rebels attacked at dawn and the fort was surrounded. Forrest called on the fort's commander, Major Bradford, to surrender. He refused. The Rebels swarmed over the fort – 231 Yankee soldiers were killed and 100 wounded. Two hundred men were also taken prisoner. A third of the POWs were black. Stories went around that the black soldiers had been massacred in cold blood and even buried alive. Other stories said wounded Yankee soldiers were burned alive in their tents. The 'Fort Pillow Massacre' was still a horror story long after the end of the war but Forrest always said it was a lie.

10a) They buried their Reb enemies there. It's now Arlington National Cemetery.

Play like a soldier

The trouble with the Civil War was it was so BORING!
Soldiers only fought for 5% of the time. They spent the
other 95% in camp. Their games included...

- Boxing, cricket (!) and baseball. Some of these baseball
  'games' could turn a bit rough and the players ended up
  badly injured – a bit like girls' netball today.

- Cock fighting. Even rougher than baseball – the loser
  ended up in the cooking pot!
- Boat racing. Not rowing but racing tiny model boats.
  They were carved from wood, had paper sails, and were
  raced down rivers. How sweet.

- Playing cards – but the preachers said it was sinful and they'd go to Hell if they died. The soldiers threw away their cards before they went into battle … then picked them up again if they survived! (Some of these cards had pictures of their generals on the back – and some Yankee cards had very rude pictures of women on the back … and they were very popular!)

Do these games sound a bit boring? Here are a couple of…

Games you wouldn't want to play

Louse racing
You need:
2–6 players and one louse from each player's hair.
One-penny entry fee per louse.
A sheet of lined paper turned up along the long edge so the lice can't run off sideways.
A whistle.

To play:
1 Place the paper on a flat surface.
2 Line up the lice on the top line, facing the bottom of the page. (You may have trouble deciding which end of a louse is its face. Hold it in your hand and stick out your tongue. If it sticks out a tongue then you have its face. If it doesn't you are probably looking at its bum.)
3 When they are all set, blow the whistle. The one that crosses the most lines is the winner.
4 The winning owner wins all the entry fees. The winning louse can be thrown on the nearest fire – it's what's called a louse-warming party.

The Civil War soldiers didn't use paper – it was too precious. They drew a race course on the side of their tents. You can try either. See which one your head lice prefer.

There were also 'Louse Battles' fought but there are no clues as to how they managed this. Did they get their enemy in a head-lock? Were the losers scalped? Was it a hair-raising event for the lice?

Pop goes the canteen
A game for simple-minded creatures who are easily amused. (Boys aged 8 to 88 are good at this.)

You need:
A metal water bottle (called a canteen).
Gunpowder.
A camp fire.

To play:
1 Put the gunpowder in the empty canteen.
2 Put the cork stopper in the canteen as tightly as possible.

3 Throw the canteen on the camp fire. The heat will make the powder explode and fire the cork out.
4 Duck.

Yes, a very childish game if the cork hits someone.

Talk like a soldier

We know a lot about the Civil War from the letters of soldiers who wrote home. But some soldiers wrote home to complain ... about the letters they got from home!

Here is a genuine Civil War letter from a soldier to his mum!

> Mother when you wright to me get somebody to write that can wright a plain hand to read. I cold not read your letter to make sence of it cos it is wrote so bad. I have lurned to do my own reading and writing and it is grate help to me. — Tom

He has a bit of a nerve complaining about his old mum's writing, doesn't he?

Another soldier wrote…

> *I believe the Doctors kill more than they cour. Doctors haint got half sence.*

And your teacher says *your* spelling is bad?

Teechas doant noh evree fingt

Here are some of the spellings the Civil War soldiers used. What do they mean?

a. dyereaer

b. accitment

c. ceepit

d. A brim ham lillkern

e. Fluriday

Answers: a) diarrhoea (the Rebs called diarrhoea the 'Virginia quickstep.'); **b)** excitement; **c)** keep it; **d)** Abraham Lincoln; **e)** Florida

Super slang

Soldiers had their own language while they were away at war. They didn't call the toilet holes 'toilets', they called them 'sinks' – but 'stinks' may have been a better word!

Some soldiers didn't like using a 'rude' word when writing home to Mom. In 1863, Private Richard Waldrop from Virginia wrote home saying that when he had got up that morning…

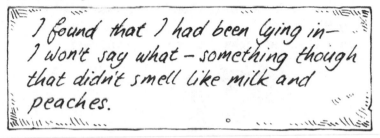

I found that I had been lying in— I won't say what – something though that didn't smell like milk and peaches.

A Civil War soldier would understand if his friend said…

OLD JAKE WAS A HUGELY CHIRK GUY TILL WE GOT INTO BATTLE. THEN HE GOT A BRICK IN HIS HAT AND SKEDADDLED. THE GENERAL DIDN'T LIKE MEN TO ABSQUATULATE SO HE SHOT HIM COLD AS A WAGON TYRE

YOU DON'T SAY?

'Chirk' is cheerful, to get 'a brick in the hat' is to get drunk and 'absquatulate' is to run away from the battle. You can work out the rest, can't you?

Southern sums

The sums in North Carolina schools were pretty bloodthirsty! During the Civil War the Reb kids did sums using 'Johnson's Elementary Arithmetic'. Here are some of the questions…

a) A Rebel soldier captured eight Yankees each day for nine days; how many did he capture in all?
b) If one Rebel soldier kills 90 Yankees, how many Yankees can ten Rebel soldiers kill?
c) If one Rebel soldier can whip seven Yankees, how many soldiers can whip 49 Yankees?

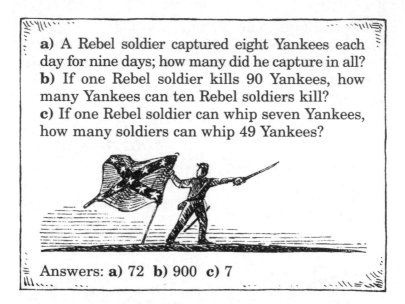

Answers: **a)** 72 **b)** 900 **c)** 7

Eat like a soldier

The soldier's food is very rough,
The bread is hard, the beef is tough.

War meant a shortage of food for many. So soldiers came up with some interesting and disgusting ways to survive...

Cream your coffee
Short of milk for your coffee? Stir in butter or egg white instead!

Suck on salt horse
Actually it is salt beef – so salty it won't rot for two years ... and so salty you can't eat it! It has to be soaked in water for hours to get rid of the salty taste. That also gets rid of *any* taste.

Chomp on chicken soup

Most soldiers hate the hospital food, especially chicken soup – which they nickname 'shadow soup'. Here's how they said it was made...

Shadow Soup

1. A chicken is hung up in the sun where its shadow would fall into the cooking pot.

2. Water is put into the cooking pot and the shadow is boiled.

3. Salt, pepper and other spices are added to make it taste of something and it is served out.

Eat beetle bread

The bread is usually so hard it has to be softened by dipping it into coffee. The warm wet coffee then loosens up the beetles that have made a home in it! One soldier said...

The only fresh meat we had was the worms and weevils in the bread!

COULD I HAVE SOME MORE COFFEE?

The soldiers nickname their bread 'Worm Castles'.

Feast on fruit

Soldiers have to grab food when they have a chance. They steal farm animals as they march through the countryside, they hunt birds and animals and they pick fruit. At the Battle of Blackburn's Ford the Yankee soldiers were being smashed by Rebs. Their Yankee friends at the back should have rushed to help them – but they were too busy picking blackberries!

Bear for brunch

Soldiers are not supposed to steal from farmers. Rebel officers will often warn their men…

The soldiers then shoot the pigs. When the officer complains the men say…

(This is a bear-faced lie, of course.) Others kill chickens and even have an excuse for that…

Relish roast rat

By the end of the war the Rebs are so hungry they buy rats or mule meat to eat. A Vicksburg woman said, 'There is nothing else to be found!'

Civil War firsts

Wars usually make inventors invent new and terrible ways of foul fighting. But which of these were first thought of in the American Civil War? Answer true or false.

Answers:

1 True. They were used by Yankees to report on Reb army movements. If the balloonists got air-sick they could always vomit on the heads of the enemy.

2 True. Both sides used spies to tap into telegraph wires and steal battle plans. They also sent false information to the enemy.

3 True. Instant coffee was given to Yankee soldiers – they hated it. This may have been where the old joke came from...

4 True. The ship called *Monitor* was the first Yankee iron ship. It's great invention was to be fitted with flushing toilets. It met up with the Rebs' only iron ship *Virginia* in a 4-hour battle. The ships were strong but the shells they fired were weak. Neither one could sink the other so the battle ended up a draw.

5 True. They carried soldiers back from battle too – to hospitals. Trains were also used to carry heavy guns into battle and saved them being dragged by poor horses. The guns went mainline instead of maneline!

6 True. On 14 April 1865 Abraham Lincoln was shot in the head as he watched a play in the theatre. This led to the ancient joke…

7 True. Some of the first photographs were taken during battle, but most Civil War photos were posed. James Gibson and Alexander Gardner took photos after the battle at Antietam. To make photos more dramatic, they moved bodies about, they arranged their arms, legs and clothes. They gave the dead weapons. (They carried one musket about with them and the same musket appears in many photos.) They were cheats.

8 True. Yankee General Gabriel James Rains invented working torpedoes. These weren't like modern torpedoes but more like floating tin cans full of gunpowder. After the war Rains claimed his torpedoes had sunk 58 Reb ships. These torpedoes were usually exploded by electrical wires from shore.

9 True. On 17 February 1864, the Reb submarine *Hunley* crossed Charleston harbour underwater to attack the Yankee ship *Housatonic* with a 100-pound torpedo. The torpedo exploded and the *Housatonic* sank … but sadly so did the submarine! The Yankees built their own submarine (powered by sailors with oars) and it sank before it even attacked a Reb ship! It was called the *Alligator*.

10 False … but almost true! Lincoln wanted the Yankees to build another submarine after the *Alligator* sank. Inventor Pascal Plant suggested a rocket-powered submarine! This was rejected but he was encouraged to build a rocket-powered torpedo. The first test worked OK. The torpedo hit a mud bank and exploded. On the second test the torpedo sank the schooner *Diana*. Sadly this was one of the Yankees' own ships. On the third test, the torpedo was fired and was seen to leave the water and fly through the air for 100 metres before it splashed back into the water. However, the Union Navy Department did not see this as the future of war but a waste of money.

Wonder weapons

Want to beat your deadly rivals but can't get past them? Then try going UNDER them! The Yankees had hundreds of coal-miners fighting for them. This was the great plan...

But what happened *after* the explosion…

Well, it seemed like a good idea at the time!

Putrid for prisoners

You're a soldier and you lose a battle. The good news is you are captured alive and sent to a Prisoner of War 'camp'. The bad news is there is more chance of dying in a prison camp than there is in a battle!

Peep into hell
At Elmira prison, New York, around one-third of the Rebel prisoners died of starvation or disease. The camp doctor told his bosses...

The camp stinks and the stream flowing through the camp has become green with pollution. There is no shelter, and no straw for bedding.

A Texas Reb prisoner wrote...

If there was ever a hell on earth Elmira prison was that hell.

But don't worry! Those Reb prisoners didn't die ignored! A local man built a platform outside the camp where, for 10 cents, locals could come and watch the Rebels suffering.

Awful Andersonville
Rebs made the Yankees suffer just as much.
- 41,000 Yankee soldiers were sent to the Reb camp at Andersonville. 13,000 died. Sometimes 100 per day.
- For the first few months the prisoners had no tools to bury the dead.

- All water came from a stream – called the Sweetwater – it was also the only sewer. Sweet, huh?
- There was little shelter – prisoners blistered in summer and froze in winter.
- If you crossed the 'deadline' five metres from the stockade – you were shot dead.

To add to Yankee misery, a gang of prisoners – called the 'Raiders' – robbed, beat and killed their fellow Yankees. That's friends for you! The Raiders boss was Willie Collins – a six-foot-tall bully. Finally, with help from the Reb guards, another group of prisoners – known as the 'Regulators' – fought the Raiders. Willie Collins was tried and sentenced to death.

Willie was strung up but the old rope broke. He was hung up for a second time. A crowd of 26,000 prisoners watched Willie and five other Raiders hang. Some chanted 'Dead, Dead, Dead!'. One prisoner swung for 27 minutes before he died.

Feeling ruff

Prisoners were badly fed and could catch fatal diseases. If they tried to escape they'd be shot. One group of Yankee prisoners found a way of surviving, as the local newspaper might have reported...

The Belle Isle and Richmond Enquirer
23 May 1862

PROTECT THOSE PETS

The people of Richmond are proud to have the Belle Isle prison camp on their doorstep. Those Yankee losers are there for all of us to see and enjoy!

Bank and Yank

They are safe behind a three-foot-high bank of earth – any Yankee who crosses it is shot on the spot. But not everything is safe from the evil enemy. Last week it was reported that the camp commander lost his dog. The prisoners whistled and called for the dog till it crossed the bank into the camp. The dog was never seen again. Guards reported that the prisoners were later seen enjoying a meaty stew!

Since then several pets have gone missing from the Richmond area. A tearful Mrs Betty York said, 'My pet poodle is probably in some Yankee pudding by now!' Undertaker George Taylforth complained, 'I fear my Buster is a German Shepherd's pie!'

So keep those pets safe in your yard. If they must go out then have them on a lead. After all, we don't want our loved ones filling Yankee bellies with spaniel soup, collie casserole amd beagle-burger, do we?

It could be stew!

The great escapes 1

If you were a prisoner in one of those awful camps you'd want to escape, wouldn't you? Some escapes were simple. Reb Private J Branch escaped from prison by bribing a Yankee guard to look the other way. He then walked back to his home in Tennessee. The bribe was $7.50.

The great escapes 2

In Libby Prison, the prisoners decided to escape by tunnel even though they only had small pocket knives to dig with.

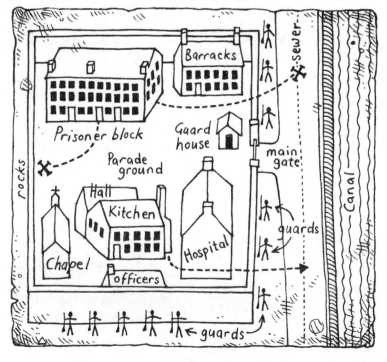

- Tunnel 1 ran into solid rock and had to be abandoned.
- Tunnel 2 aimed to cut into a sewer under the street between the prison and the canal but the tunnel flooded.
- Tunnel 3 – dug in January 1864 – started behind a kitchen fireplace, went down a chimney and into a cellar under the hospital. From there a 17-metre tunnel was planned to go under the heavily guarded street. The work took 17 days. On the night of the escape, 109 men slipped down the chimney and into the tunnel. The last few feet of soil were removed ... but the tunnel was too short – it ended in the middle of the street!

But the Rebel guards were so surprised they simply watched as the prisoners popped up out of the ground and ran into the night.

Of the 109, 58 were recaptured, two drowned, but 49 got back home. The original escape planner Colonel Frederick Bartleson did NOT escape – why not?

a) He was too scared of being caught and shot.
b) He was too fat to go down the chimney.
c) He got lost.

Answer: b) Perhaps Fat Freddy needed lessons from Fat Father Christmas!

Warring women

The American Civil War was tough on the soldiers, but many people forget women were just as much part of the war. It is reckoned that 400 fighting females, dressed as men, fought in the Civil War and other women found different ways to fight too...

Loreta Janeta Valazuquez

Identity: Born in Cuba and brought up in New Orleans.

Record: - Loreta, dressed as Lieutenant Harry T Bulford, fought for the Rebs at the First Battle of Manassas.
- She wore a fake beard and wore a wire frame under her uniform to give her the shape of a man.
- She had a black servant called Bob - who didn't know his master was a woman.
- Later Loreta dressed as a woman and went to Washington to spy, where she met President Lincoln.

End: She returned to fighting - her first love - and was wounded.

Belle Boyd

Identity: 17-year-old Reb beauty from Virginia.

Record:
- When war started Belle flew a Rebel flag over her home. When a Yankee soldier tried to take it down she shot him.
- Belle went on to use her good looks to chat up Yankee soldiers. While they cuddled they told her their secrets.
- In 1862 she was arrested and put on a train for Baltimore. She spent the entire trip waving a Rebel flag out of the window. In Baltimore, she was jailed - in the local hotel. She sang Rebel songs day and night. Eventually she was sent South - probably to get rid of her.
- When she went on a spy ship she was captured again but chatted up a sailor - made a change from a soldier - and escaped to Canada then England (where she married the sailor!)

End: She returned to the USA and toured with a one-woman show about her adventures. Died 1900.

Crazy Bet and Mary Elizabeth

Identity: *Elizabeth Van Lew (also known as Crazy Bet) lived near Libby Prison in Richmond. Mary Elizabeth Bowzer was a slave of the Van Lew family*

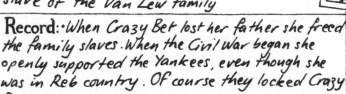

Record: •When Crazy Bet lost her father she freed the family slaves. When the Civil War began she openly supported the Yankees, even though she was in Reb country. Of course they locked Crazy Bet away.
• Crazy Bet still got spy messages in and out of Libby Prison using plates with false bottoms or coded in pin pricks in the pages of books.
• Her greatest success was through her ex-slave Mary Elizabeth, whom she 'rented' to the Reb President. Mary Bowzer could read and write, she was clever and her new owners never suspected her of helping Crazy Bet to spy.
• Mary Elizabeth spied in on meetings, copied down messages and looked at maps. All the information made its way back to the Yankees. She also dug up bodies of soldiers and sent them back to their families!
• Mary Elizabeth even set fire to the Reb President's house! At the end of the war the Reb President tried to flee — so Mary Elizabeth stole his wife's horse and saddle, hoping to stop them escaping!

End: Crazy Bet probably died around 1900. It's not known when Mary Elizabeth died.

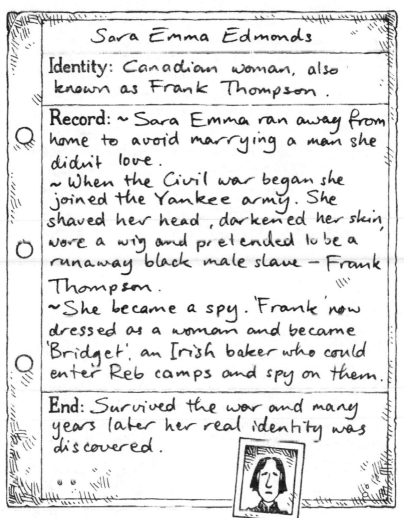

Sara Emma Edmonds

Identity: Canadian woman, also known as Frank Thompson.

Record: ~ Sara Emma ran away from home to avoid marrying a man she didn't love.
~ When the Civil war began she joined the Yankee army. She shaved her head, darkened her skin, wore a wig and pretended to be a runaway black male slave – Frank Thompson.
~ She became a spy. 'Frank' now dressed as a woman and became 'Bridget', an Irish baker who could enter Reb camps and spy on them.

End: Survived the war and many years later her real identity was discovered.

Nasty for nurses

Women served as nurses in the Civil War and had to face the same disgusting sights that the male doctors faced.

Kate Cummings was born in Edinburgh, but moved to Alabama as a child in 1835. When the Civil War started she worked as nurse for the Rebs. Kate blamed surgeons for horrors in hospitals:

115

> *A stream of blood ran from the table into a tub in which was the arm. It had been taken off at the socket and the hand was hanging over the edge of the tub, a lifeless thing. I wish I could become as heartless as the surgeons seem to be, for there is no end to these horrors.*

But it wasn't only the nurses who were shocked by what they saw. A Yankee officer said:

> *The surgeons were stripped to the waist and covered in blood. Their assistants held down the poor fellows and armed with long bloody knives and saws, cut and sawed away with frightful speed, throwing the mangled arms and legs on to a pile as soon as they were removed. The sight was too much for many of my men who vomited in their saddles when they passed by.*

After the Battle of Gettysburg one soldier said that the hospitals cut off so many arms and legs they were thrown on to piles almost two metres high.

Would you have wanted to have your wounded arm or leg cut off? Amazingly many soldiers did, their pain was so severe. A surgeon said:

> *Oh, it is awful! Poor fellows come and beg, almost on their knees for the first chance to have an arm taken off. It is a scene of horror such as I never saw. God forbid that I should see another.*

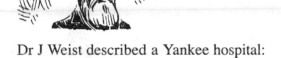

Dr J Weist described a Yankee hospital:

> Wounded men are lying everywhere. What a horrible sight they present! Here the bones of a leg or arm have been shattered like glass by a ball. Here a great hole has been torn in a stomach by a cannon shot. Nearby see that blood and froth covering the chest of one choking with blood from a wound of the lungs. By his side this beardless boy with his right leg remaining attached to his body by a few strands of blackened flesh. This one's lower jaw has been carried entirely away... The faces of some are black with powder, others are blanched with thirst and many suffer horrible pain, yet there are few groans or complaints.

That's war. That's what the Rebs and Yanks did to one another.

POTTY PRESIDENTS

The Americans weren't very keen on being ruled by King George – or King Anybody for that matter. Instead they decided to vote for their top banana and call him President. The US President is supposed to be the most powerful person on earth these days. The problem is presidents are only human. And human beings do all sorts of silly, cruel and embarrassing things.

Here are ten true tales.

1 President Abraham Lincoln (1861–65) Did you know ... he grew his famous beard at the suggestion of an 11-year-old girl who wrote to him. She said...

2 President Benjamin Harrison (1889–93) Ben was so small he was known as 'Little Ben'. One day a visitor called to see the President but he was stopped by a secretary...

Electric lights were fitted in the White House while Benjamin Harrison was president. He and Mrs Harrison were so terrified of touching the switches that they often slept with all the lights on.

3 President James A Garfield (1881) This clever clogs was 'ambidextrous' – he could use both hands to write. Many people can, but Garfield could write in Latin with one hand and in Greek with the other … at the same time! Unfortunately, neither hand could save him when he was shot by a madman.

4 President Grover Cleveland (1885–89 and 1893–97) Cleveland was accused of having a girlfriend who had a baby son, but he didn't marry her. Shocking thing in those days. His enemies made up a song: 'Ma, Ma, where's my pa?' to disgrace him. The idea was that shocked Americans would not vote for him. But they did! After Cleveland won the election, his friends changed the words to…

5 President Andrew Jackson (1829–37) Jackson was known as 'a man of the people'… but they were pretty rough people! He held a party in the White House after his election. Guests were invited in off the streets and told to entertain themselves. They did. Their 'entertainment' included:
- breaking china
- breaking glasses
- breaking windows
- standing on chairs with muddy boots
- destroying sofas
- pulling down curtains
- fighting
- getting drunk

Jackson eventually escaped through a window and spent his first night as President in a hotel. Did he learn his lesson? Not really! When Jackson was about to leave office at the end of his term, the New York State dairymen presented him with a four-foot-long, 1,400-pound cheese.

He couldn't eat it all, so what did he do? He had another White House party. The cheese was trodden into the rug and smashed into the furniture. The furniture smelled dreadful for a very long time … unless you were a White House white mouse, of course.

6 President Gerald Ford (1974–77) Queen Elizabeth II of Britain was visiting the White House and the President invited her to dance. As they stepped out on to the dance floor the orchestra played 'The Lady is a Tramp'. As Queen Victoria may have said…

7 President Lyndon Baines Johnson (1963–69) This comical character should have been on the stage. One of his habits was to hold his hound dog, Yooky, by the ears and the two would sing together.

8 President William Henry Harrison (1841) Harrison won the President's job then gave the longest-ever opening speech – 8,445 words! That's a short book and it took him a long time. He was speaking in a cruel March wind without a coat or hat – as a result of this stunt, he caught pneumonia and died a month later.

9 President Theodore Roosevelt (1901–9) Unlike Harrison, Roosevelt was saved by his speech! He was shot by a gunman just before giving a speech in Milwaukee, Wisconsin, but he decided to carry on with the speech. He said…

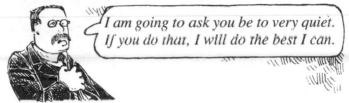

I am going to ask you be to very quiet. If you do that, I will do the best I can.

Roosevelt went ahead and gave an 80-minute speech. He was then taken to the hospital, where X-rays showed that the bullet had hit the thick script of his speech, then bounced off his glasses case in his pocket, and finally ended up in his ribcage. His doctor said, 'No doubt about it. His speech saved his life.'

10 President William Taft (1909–13) Taft was so fat that he once got stuck in the White House bath. After that, he ordered a giant tub specially made for his fat butt. It was large enough to hold *four* normal-sized men.

BUT IT'S LARGE ENOUGH TO HOLD F OUT!

Taft's Secretary of War, Elihu Root, once sent him a message asking about the President's health. Taft wrote back to say that he was so much better that he had just taken a 25-mile horseback ride. Root replied...

Deadly dream

The first US President to be assassinated was Abraham Lincoln. But the interesting thing is he should have known better! He was warned...

President Lincoln woke with a start. His eyes were wild; they stared out from grey, weary sockets. He gave a soft, long groan.

Mary Lincoln stood at the door to his bedroom and narrowed her mean little mouth. 'What's wrong, Mr Lincoln?' she asked her husband.

'Oh, Mary,' he said, shaking his shaggy head then rubbing his face with bony hands. 'Do you believe you can see the future in dreams?'

She snorted. 'Stuff and nonsense, Mr Lincoln! Stuff and nonsense! What sort of dream have you had?'

'A dream of death, Mary,' he told her. The President looked around the room. 'It was so real! It all started here. I knew I was in bed asleep but then I dreamed that I woke up. When I listened carefully I heard wailing and weeping coming from downstairs. I got out of bed to see what was happening.'

Mary Lincoln pulled the heavy curtains open and let the weak morning light fall on the ashen man in the bed. 'You should be happy, Mr Lincoln. The Civil War is won and you are the hero of the north!'

He tried to smile but his face showed more pain than happiness. 'In my dream I went downstairs here and looked in every room. They were all empty. At last I came to the East Room and it was guarded by two soldiers. I looked through the door and there were all my friends gathered around the table sobbing.'

Mary's moon face was troubled now. 'What were they sobbing about?'

'They were gathered around a coffin. There was a body in the coffin, dressed in funeral clothes. I couldn't make out his face because it was covered with a cloth. So I turned and asked a soldier who had died.'

'Who was it?' the President's wife asked.

He turned his great eyes on his wife and said, 'The soldier told me it was President Lincoln in that coffin ... and he'd been shot by an assassin! It was me, Mary. Me!'

The woman's sour lips twisted in scorn. 'Stuff and nonsense. No one would want to shoot the hero of the war – the great President Lincoln,' she sneered and there was spite in her words. Jealousy.

'The south lost the war,' he reminded her. 'I'm not a hero in the south!'

'They would gain nothing by shooting you now – during the war maybe. But not now. You're safe. Now stir yourself and get out of bed. Remember we go to the theatre tonight. The people want to see their hero President.'

'Yes, dear,' he said wearily.

The people saw little of their president that night. He sat in a small room that overlooked the stage. He sat back in the shadows in a rocking chair and watched the play wearily.

It was a comedy, *Our American Cousin*. The audience were enjoying it. Even Mary laughed. But Abraham Lincoln was tired to the core of his bones and the horror of his morning's dream made the shadows around him deeper.

And from those deep shadows stepped a man. If that stranger had been on the stage the audience would have cheered him. He was John Wilkes Booth, one of America's most popular actors. Booth's hand tightened over the pistol in his hand. He couldn't believe his luck.

He had crept up the stairs to this room. The President's guard had grown bored and slipped away for a drink. When Booth tried the door it had been unlocked. He'd opened it silently and now he stood a pace behind the man he hated. The man who'd defeated his beloved South. President Abe Lincoln.

The President and his guests looked down on the brightly lit stage. The actor on the stage called to another, 'You sockdologizing old mantrap!' The audience roared with laughter.

That was the moment Booth had waited for. He knew the play. He had timed it so he would arrive here at this very moment. Now he raised the pistol, placed it behind the President's ear and pulled the trigger.

The small gun wasn't as loud as the cheering audience. At first Mary Lincoln didn't realize what had happened. All she knew was that a man rushed past her and jumped up to the ledge that overlooked the stage. 'Freedom for the South!' he cried before he jumped down.

The audience were confused. This wasn't part of the plot, was it? Some laughed, some gasped and some fell silent.

As the strange man with the gun limped off the stage they turned their eyes to the balcony where a moon-faced woman looked down on them and screamed, 'The President! Mr Lincoln! He's been shot!'

Mary Lincoln turned and fell on her knees beside the lifeless man in the rocking chair. In the uproar that followed no one heard her whisper, 'Oh, the dream, Mr Lincoln! The dream!'

President Lincoln died the following morning. John Wilkes Booth was caught ten days later and died in a gunfight with the soldiers sent to arrest him.

Since that day there have been reports that the ghost of Abe Lincoln wanders through the White House...

That may or may not be true. But one thing seems pretty certain – Abe Lincoln reported that he'd had a dream in which he saw that he'd been shot by an assassin.

And that dream came true.

Did you know...?
President Lincoln was the first US President to be assassinated, and in 1963 John F Kennedy became the latest. There are some curiously creepy facts that link the two murders...

- Lincoln died from a bullet to the head while he sat next to his wife in the Ford Theatre. Kennedy died from a bullet to the head while he sat next to his wife in a Ford car.
- Lincoln was succeeded by his vice-president, a man called Johnson. Kennedy was succeeded by *his* vice-president, a man called Johnson.
- Lincoln's killer shot the President in a theatre and hid in a storeroom. Kennedy's killer shot the President from a storeroom and hid in a theatre.
- Lincoln's killer was shot dead before he could stand trial. Kennedy's killer was shot dead before *he* could stand trial.
- Lincoln's killer was known by three names (John Wilkes Booth) and those three names have fifteen letters.

Kennedy's killer was also known by three names (Lee Harvey Oswald) and those three names have fifteen letters too.

Spooky, eh?

Dreadful doctors

The worst thing a US President could do was go to the doctor. If you ever become US President and fall sick then stay sick. You may die. But if you call in a deadly doctor you'll *certainly* die. Look at what they've done...

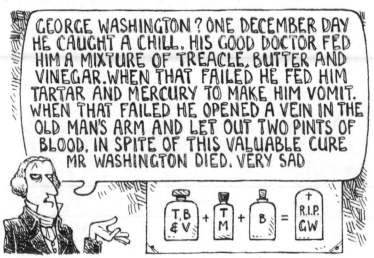

GEORGE WASHINGTON? ONE DECEMBER DAY HE CAUGHT A CHILL. HIS GOOD DOCTOR FED HIM A MIXTURE OF TREACLE, BUTTER AND VINEGAR. WHEN THAT FAILED HE FED HIM TARTAR AND MERCURY TO MAKE HIM VOMIT. WHEN THAT FAILED HE OPENED A VEIN IN THE OLD MAN'S ARM AND LET OUT TWO PINTS OF BLOOD. IN SPITE OF THIS VALUABLE CURE MR WASHINGTON DIED. VERY SAD

T.B & V + T M + B = R.I.P. G.W

The treacle, butter and vinegar almost killed the old man. The mercury *should* have done because it's a poison! Of course we now know that the 'blood-letting' cure is useless and probably killed him more quickly!

PRESIDENT LINCOLN? HE WAS SHOT WITH A SINGLE BULLET THAT ENTERED BEHIND HIS EAR AND LODGED IN HIS BRAIN. THE PRESIDENT WAS UNCONSCIOUS

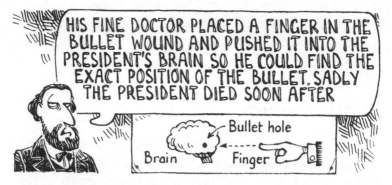

Of course he died, you idiot! The doctor probably pushed the bullet deeper into the brain and finished him off. Lincoln might not have recovered – but his doctor never gave him a chance.

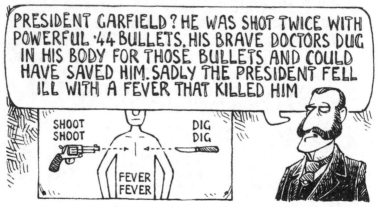

And where did the President get the fever? He was treated with the most modern treatment: the 'Nelaton Probe', a metal instrument which was pushed into the wound and turned slowly to find the track of a bullet. The probe missed the track in Garfield's case, and became painfully stuck in his ribcage. The doctor had to dig the probe out with his fingers. Garfield died on 17 September 1881, of infection … not the assassin's bullet. He got that infection from the dirty instruments and unwashed hands of his scruffy doctors!

LEGENDS AND LIES

In US history there have been lots of famous people who are supposed to have done lots of famous things. Sadly a lot of these stories are about as real as Cinderella's slippers and the tales are as tall as Jack's beanstalk.

Here are a few TRUE facts about these fantastic fictions...

George Washington's chopped cherry

The tall tale

The simple truth

This story was first told in 1806 – seven years after Georgie died – in a book written by Parson Weems. Most of the stories, like the cherry tree, were made up. The US people wanted to believe them so the book became a best-seller and the cherry-tree tale became 'true'. (Even Parson Weems wasn't true! Mason Locke Weems called himself 'Parson of Mount Vernon Parish' but there is no such parish.)

Davy Crockett – Old Betsy bashing

The tall tale

Davy Crockett
The hero who died fighting
for his country

Davy Crockett was born in the frontier woods of Tennessee. He grew up as a poor but loyal Indian-fighter and brave bear-killer.

When duty called he went to Texas to fight with the Texas rebels against Mexican rule. He picked up his racoon-skin cap and his rifle, 'Old Betsy', and set off to defend our wonderful country. The Texans were struggling to free themselves from their Mexican masters and needed all the help they could get.

In April 1836 the 3,000-man Mexican army attacked the brave 180 Texas defenders at the Alamo fort. On 6 March, after a 13-day struggle, the Mexicans broke through. The gallant Texans fought to the last man ... and that last man was Davy Crockett. When the Tennessee man ran out of bullets he used his gun as a club. He never gave up and died a true US hero.

We can all learn a lesson from Davy: 'Never give up!'

The simple truth

He was certainly an Indian-fighter and bear-killer – he says
he once killed 105 bears in six months for their skins.
(Goldilocks would have loved him!) He battled through
flooded rivers to get more powder and shot, and then
returned to kill still more bears.

But he didn't spend all his time in the wild woods. He
was elected to the US Congress and went off to
Washington to be a politician. In Washington his friends
built up the stories of his simple courage – 'He killed him
a bear when he was only three!' But then he was voted
OUT of Congress and Davy was a bit put out. In fact he
was so upset he went off to Texas to massacre Mexicans
and work off some of his anger.

He DID die at the Alamo ... but did he go down fighting
bravely? Probably NOT! A diary of Mexican officer Jose
Enrique de la Pena was translated into English in 1970 and
it mentions the 'execution' of Crockett. Jose says...

> *Crockett was recognized among the*
> *survivors. There was an argument*
> *among our Mexican officers as to what*
> *we should do with them. Some officers*
> *pushed themselves to the front so the*

131

> general would notice their bravery. These officers took their swords in their hands and fell upon these unfortunate and defenceless men just like a tiger leaps on his prey. They were tortured before they were killed but these men died without complaining.

Crockett's body was soaked in oil and burned.

So there it is. Crockett died bravely – along with others – but he was captured alive and didn't die swinging Old Betsy the way the films and books tell it.

Wyatt Earp, fastest gun in the West

The tall tale

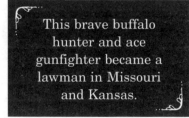
This brave buffalo hunter and ace gunfighter became a lawman in Missouri and Kansas.

After cleaning up those states, honest Wyatt headed for his greatest challenge – to bring law to Tombstone, Arizona.

The simple truth

Wyatt Earp was a liar, horse-thief, stagecoach robber and killer. He was born in Kentucky in 1848. Only Newton, the eldest of the six Earp boys, kept out of trouble. The others – James, Virgil, Wyatt, Morgan and Warren – were all bad.

In 1870 Wyatt was elected town constable of Lamar, Missouri. In 1871 he was accused of stealing two horses. Earp raised $500 bail and then fled. In the 1870s Wyatt worked as a barman and was a gambler and a cheat – in the book he wrote about his life he claimed that he had been an Indian fighter and buffalo hunter, plus part-time lawman.

133

Moving to Wichita, Wyatt became a policeman until he was dismissed for fighting. He later claimed to have cleaned up the town! Wyatt then moved to Dodge, where he later claimed he had been Marshal, bringing law and order to the town. Not true. He was a policeman for a few months but only arrested a few drunks.

In 1877 Wyatt was in Fort Griffin where he teamed up with gambler and part-time dentist John 'Doc' Holliday and his partner 'Big Nose' Kate Elder. Holliday was dying from tuberculosis and alcoholism but was still feared – he had once cut a man's throat during a row over a poker game!

By 1879, Wyatt with his brothers and Holliday were in the tough town of Tombstone and were soon suspected of cattle-stealing (rustling) and stagecoach-robbing, plus cheating at cards. In their spare time they acted as armed bouncers for saloons.

In 1881 a bungled stagecoach robbery left two people dead. No one knows for sure whether the Earps or the Clanton gang had taken part but it seems that the two families fell out about it. This led to the 'Gunfight at the OK Corral'– a row between thieves over a robbery, not lawmen going after bad men!

In October 1881, Ike Clanton and Tom McLaury went into town for supplies. That night Holliday dared Clanton to reach for his gun. Clanton wasn't carrying a gun – so he survived a little longer! The next day witnesses saw Wyatt Earp hit McLaury (even though he was unarmed) with his favourite long-barrelled revolver, the 'Buntline Special'. This is what *really* happened next...

ON 26 OCTOBER, 1881, FRANK AND TOM McLAURY, IKE AND BILLY CLANTON PLUS BILLY CLAIBOURNE WERE AT THE OK CORRAL PREPARING TO LEAVE TOWN

ONLY BILL CLANTON AND FRANK HAD REVOLVERS

THEN DOWN THE STREET CAME WYATT, VIRGIL AND MORGAN EARP PLUS DOC HOLLIDAY

ALL WITH REVOLVERS AND SHOTGUNS

The OK Corral incident was NOT a gunfight. It was mass murder. And the Earps got away with it.

- Later that year, Virgil was shot and crippled for life – he died in 1905.
- In 1882 Morgan was shot dead playing billiards. The Earps murdered the man who planned Morgan's killing.
- Warren was shot by a cowboy he had bullied.
- Wyatt Earp gave interviews that built up his legend as a fearless lawman. He died in 1929. Two years later 'Wyatt Earp: Frontier Marshal' (untrue!) was published. One newspaper, however, called him the 'Tombstone Terror'. (True.)

Billy the Kid – tiny terror

The tall tale

The simple truth

Sheriff Pat Garrett was an old drinking pal of Billy the Kid. He was ordered to capture Billy – which he did. Garrett then decided to cash in on his famous action by writing the life story of Billy. With Ash Upson he wrote *The Authentic Life of Billy the Kid*. But Billy's life was pretty boring so he made up some of the facts and didn't check others. People still believe Garrett's stories, but the truth is…

- Billy's real name was NOT William H Bonney. That was the name Billy invented for himself when he was on the run from jail in New Mexico. He was known as Kid Antrim, but his real name was Henry McCarty.
- He did NOT kill his first victim when he was 12. Billy was 18 when he killed a blacksmith called 'Windy' Cahill after an argument. Billy didn't even own a gun and killed him with Windy's own gun. His life of crime started with the glorious theft of some laundry!
- Billy did NOT kill 21 people before he was 21. He probably killed eight at the most in his whole life.
- Billy was NOT a handsome hero. He was most famous for his rabbit teeth – a sort of Bugs Bunny with a pistol.

In fact Henry McCarty, a.k.a. Billy the Kid, was just one big loser.

Just before Christmas 1880, Billy plus four friends were trapped in a shepherd's hut by Sheriff Pat Garrett and his posse at Stinking Springs.

One of the gang was shot dead before the others surrendered. After his trial Billy was sentenced to death but he killed two prison guards and escaped. Garrett hunted Billy for another three months before he finally killed him in an ambush.

Garrett was eventually killed by Wayne Brazil, who was tried for murder but set free. Maybe Brazil and the judge didn't like Garrett's book!

THE WICKED WILD WEST

The roughest and toughest Americans went out West where there was still land to be grabbed and fortunes to be made. In the new towns of the Wild West even the lawmen were lawless and gun-slinging outlaws got away with murder.

Wild quiz

Could you be the fastest quiz shot in the West? (Or the East, South or North?) Here are ten terribly hard questions for your brain cell. If you can't manage then ask a teacher to spare their brain cell (if they have one). Answer true or false...

1 Wild Bill Longley was shot by vigilantes and the shooting saved his life.
2 John Wesley Hardin killed 43 men and was a Sunday school teacher.

3 Tom Horn made the rope he was hanged with.
4 The Dalton gang didn't wear masks, they wore false beards when they robbed a bank.

5 Lawmen could capture villains dead or alive, but they preferred them dead.

6 Cowboys hated sheep but they would never harm them.

7 Wild West wild man Bill Rigney was lynched even though he was close to death at the time.

8 Saloon-bar singer Belle Starr lived a rough life but became a nun and died peacefully.

9 'Little Britches' Stephens escaped being shot because 'Little Britches' was a woman.

10 Stagecoach robber Black Bart wore black.

Answers:

1 True. Killer William Preston 'Wild Bill' Longley was captured by vigilantes along with a horse thief, Tom Johnson. Both were hung from a tree. As the vigilantes rode off, the vigilantes fired shots back at the swinging men. One bullet cut the rope and Wild Bill fell to the ground, still alive. (He left Tom to hang! Nice man.) Bill was finally hanged again in 1878, aged 27, and this time there were 4,000 spectators at his execution. After he had hung for 11 minutes, doctors announced he was dead. But legend soon grew that Bill had survived, that he had bribed a doctor to rig a harness under his shirt to prevent the noose from working. Bill had then escaped to South America. When the ship *Lusitania* was sunk in 1915, one of the passengers was ' W P Longley' from South America. Did Wild Bill survive hanging *twice*?

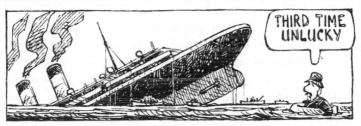

2 True. Hardin killed anyone who got in his way – only six of his victims were gunfighters. He once crawled under a tent to sneak in to see a circus. When the doorman tried to stop him Hardin shot the man – and he wasn't clowning. Hardin was eventually caught and was sentenced to 25 years in prison. In prison he studied law and ran the prison Sunday school. He was released after 16 years and settled as a lawyer in El Paso. In 1895 Hardin was drinking in a saloon when he was shot in the back of the head. His killer – John Selman – was set free. He claimed he shot Hardin in self-defence.

3 True. Tom Horn was a lawman who became an outlaw. In 1880 he had a job as a detective sent to track down train robbers. Many he simply killed. He always left his calling card – a rock placed under each victim's head. By the 1890s he had become a self-employed assassin, working for cattle ranchers and killing off their rivals. In 1902, he killed 14-year-old Willie Nickell, son of a shepherd, as a warning to his father. He was tried and hanged in November 1903. He twisted the rope himself. A photo of him making the rope was taken and proved to be a best-seller!

4 True. In 1892 the Dalton Gang rode into the town of Coffeyville to rob its bank. As they were well-known in town, they were wearing false whiskers as disguises. It didn't work! They were immediately recognized, and when the robbers came out of the bank, the Marshal and his men were ready for them. Grat Dalton was badly wounded in the gun battle, but as he fell he shot dead the Marshal who had shot him. Before Grat could do any more damage John Kloehr – the president of the local rifle club – shot him through the neck. Bob Dalton (the leader) had also been shot but continued to fire, leaning against a barn. The ever-helpful Kloehr shot him in the chest. Emmet Dalton was hit 16 times but recovered. He was the only survivor from the gang. He went to prison for life and died in 1937.

SAY! ISN'T THAT EMMET DALTON?

5 False. Lawmen would usually lose any reward or expenses if an outlaw was killed. Then, if no one claimed the corpse, the lawman had to pay for the burial too. So no lawman killed unless he was forced to. (Killing the murderer Jason Labreu cost Deputy Fannin $60.) Judge Parker paid lawmen 6 cents per mile for tracking an outlaw, $2 arrest fee, plus 10 cents per mile to feed and transport the outlaw back to justice.

6 False. In 1880 Texas cowboys cut the throats of 240 sheep. In 1887, 2,600 were burnt alive. This was part of the 'Range Wars', where the cattlemen fought shepherds for precious land.

7 True. In 1883, in Miles City, Montana, Charlie Brown was a popular saloon keeper. Troublemaker Bill Rigney came into Charlie's saloon and became very drunk. He began to insult the wife and daughter of a local man. Charlie cracked him over the head and Rigney fell to the floor, dying. Charlie could hang for his murder and the local people didn't want that! So they quickly formed a vigilante committee and lynched the dying Rigney so Charlie couldn't be blamed for killing him!

8 False. Belle often dressed as a man to commit her crimes – one of the nastiest was when she helped raid an Indian's home and used torture to discover the hiding-place of gold coins. At the age of 41 she got into an argument with a man who then shot her in the back. As she fell to the ground he shot her in the face. She kept nice company, didn't she? Belle was a member of several outlaw gangs and saw her two outlaw husbands gunned down.

9 True. Jennie Stephens was aged just 16 and from a respectable family when she met Bill Doolin (of Bill Dalton's gang) at a dance. She followed him back to the gang's hideout, where she worked in a kitchen and on the farm, doing some rustling from time to time. In 1894, when most of Dalton's gang were killed or captured, Jennie was tracked down and trapped in a farmhouse. She jumped from a window and rode for safety. She was chased by a lawman, who shot her horse because he could not shoot a woman.

After a struggle she was captured and the lawman then spanked her! She went to prison for two years and died of tuberculosis not long after her release. Not all women were so lucky. Fat Ella Watson – alias Cattle Kate – bought and sold stolen cattle. She was hanged by vigilantes for cattle stealing in 1889.

10 False. In the 1870s Black Bart was a well-dressed gentleman who dressed in a black bowler hat and black suit. But when he robbed stages he wore a long white coat and a white flour sack over his head with eye-holes cut in it. He only ever said four words – 'Throw down the box!' What did he say when he pinched the flour sack from a baker? 'Give me the dough?' (Flour … dough … geddit? Oh, never mind.) Bart's other odd habit was leaving poems at the scenes of his crimes. His first read…

> *I've laboured long and hard for bread,*
> *For honour and for riches,*
> *But on my corns too long you've tred,*
> *You fine-haired sons of bitches.*
> *Black Bart, the poet*

Bart was caught and turned out to be an elderly, respectable gentleman.

Lawless lawmen

Some of the Wild West characters were not all they seemed ... and not at all like John Wayne or Clint Eastwood in the movies. In fact, sometimes the sheriffs and judges were the worst crooks of all!

Henry Plummer
Henry began work in the 1850s when he killed the husband of a woman he fancied. (Sending her flowers would have been a less messy way to show his love.)

After the usual career of killings and robberies, he was elected sheriff of Bannock, Montana in 1863. 'Set a thief to catch a thief' they say! By then he ran an army of 200 outlaws called 'The Innocents'. Their favourite trick was robbing coaches carrying gold, which had been specially marked with chalk by an accomplice.

He was finally betrayed by some of his gang in 1864. He asked his townspeople: 'You wouldn't hang your own sheriff, would you?' They did. Twenty-four other Innocents were also hung.

WHY ARE YOU HANGING ME ? 'COS YOU'RE AN INNOCENT MAN!

Wild Bill Hickok
James Butler Hickok was born in 1837, in Illinois, the son of a preacher. He was a liar and a boaster. He gave himself the nickname 'Wild Bill', but others called him 'Duck Bill' because of his big droopy nose and jutting lips. He tried to hide these under a large moustache.

He worked for a freight firm and managed Rock Creek Station. When three farmers went to the station to complain about not being paid for land they had sold, Hickok shot them. They were all unarmed. Hickok later claimed that he had been attacked by nine gunmen. He was tried and acquitted of murder.

During the Civil War, Hickok served as a Northern spy. In 1865 he had become a professional gambler in Missouri. By 1869 he was sheriff of Fort Hays. He enforced a local law about carrying weapons by patrolling the streets armed with a sawn-off shotgun, two revolvers, a derringer and a Bowie knife. He now dressed in fancy buckskins or velvet with a red sash and a huge sombrero. The legend was being made.

In 1870, he killed four soldiers in a saloon brawl and fled the town. When he next appeared it was as marshal of Abilene. He killed two men on his first day! He later shot his own deputy by mistake. After a year, he was forced to leave town.

After spells in Wild West shows, in 1876 he was sitting playing poker in Deadwood, not as he usually did with his back to a solid wall but with his back to the door. Jack McCall walked into the saloon and shot Hickok in the back of the head. Hickok now became the stuff of legends, held up as one of the USA's greatest lawmen!

Bean and gone
In 1903 the famous Judge Roy Bean died. A newspaper report of his death might have looked like this…

The Western Tribune

16 March 1903

JUDGE ROY BEAN DEAD!

A bit of the old Wild West died yesterday when Judge Roy Bean bit the dust. Bean was born in Kentucky, and left for New Orleans with slave traders aged 16. He opened a bar but soon had to flee when he shot dead a drunken Mexican.

Young Roy joined the Californian gold rush and worked for another brother as a barman until he was jailed for shooting a man and his horse during a drunken horseback duel. He escaped from jail and went back to bar work until 1858 when he had to flee for his life again and only narrowly escaped being lynched. (It was a problem with a local 'lady'.)

During the Civil War Bean led a small band of Rebel guerrillas who called themselves the 'Free Rovers' but were labelled the 'Forty Thieves'. After the war, Bean worked at a variety of jobs – cotton smuggler, Indian fighter, butcher and petty swindler.

In 1882 he began setting up travelling tent saloons for crews laying rail tracks.

At Eagle's Nest in Texas he was actually appointed Justice of the Peace. Still running his tent saloon, his 'jail' was a tree to which he chained the criminals!

In 1882 he moved to Vinegarroon (named after the local scorpions) and built a saloon. This he named 'Jersey Lilly', after the actress Lillie Langtry – his spelling was never very good. Bean's court was held on the saloon porch beneath a sign claiming him to be 'The Only Law West of the Pecos'.

The town changed its name to Langtry and grew. Miss Lillie even sent the Judge a pair of silver-plated revolvers which he used as hammers to get order in court. There are arguments over how many people Bean had executed – figures range from zero to 23 shootings plus many more hangings. One of his favourite punishments was to order the guilty prisoner to buy drinks for everyone in the saloon.

Planted Bean

Thanks to this great man the West was a safer place – unless you happened to be a victim, of course.

All of which has nothing to do with the old joke…

HEARD ABOUT JUSTICE SMITH THE JUDGE? LOST HIS CLOTHES IN A POKER GAME!

YUP! NOW THEY CALL HIM JUSTICE UNDERPANTS!

Vicious vigilantes

If you're not happy with your local lawmen then why not take the law into your own hands? Form a sort of no-nonsense Neighbourhood Watch. Arm yourselves with guns and ropes (for hanging suspects) and call yourselves 'vigilantes'.

That's what a lot of Americans did in the 1800s...

- Vigilantes in Montana hanged 30 men and terrorized many more. They would wear masks and call on suspected criminals in the middle of the night.
- In 1851 San Francisco citizens set up their own 'Committee of Vigilance', giving themselves power to hold trials and execute.
- Their first victim was John Jenkins, who was caught carrying a small safe – not his own. After a quick trial he was hanged in the street – and a huge crowd gathered to cheer.

- Soon the 'Committee' had tried 89 suspects – hanged four, publicly whipped 11, deported 28, and released 41 – before they declared San Francisco safe.

The mad, bad Benders

One of the most terrible tales of the Wild West was that of the wicked Bender family! They disappeared after their hideous habits were discovered. No one knows what happened to them after they were chased by a posse.

If one of the posse ever wrote a report on the incident it may have looked like this...

TOP SECRET

REPORT ON THE CRUEL CRIMES AND DREADFUL DEATHS OF THE BENDERS

Report by Luke Duke (only to be opened in the event of my death)

I guess the story started in the fall of 1873 when the sheriff dropped by.

'Luke!' my wife cried as I sat in my rocking chair picking my toenails. 'Luke!'

'Look at what?' I asked her and spat some toenail at the old dog by the fire. I meant to hit the fire, you understand, but I missed and hit the old dog. Serves him right for hogging the fire.

'Luke!' she said for a third time. 'That's your name!'

'So it is,' I said. 'What d'you want, woman?' (I call her woman cos I can't rightly remember her name. Could be Sarah, could be Jane, could be neither.)

'There's a tap on the door!' she said and looked scareder than a turkey when it sees an axe on Thanksgiving Day!

'A tap on the door? Funny place to put a tap,' I muttered and picked a big hunk of nail off my big toe. Tasted just fine. Better than my woman's cooking anyway.

'Answer the door, Luke!' she said.

I sighed and pulled my boot on and walked to the door. The sheriff stood there. 'Howdy, Luke!' he said.

'How did he look?' I said and scratched my head with the toenail. 'How did who look?'

'I said "Howdy, Luke," – that's your name!'

'That's my name – don't wear it out. Now what can I do for you, Sheriff?' I asked him, polite as pie.

'I need a few good men to make up a posse!' he said.

'I got a dog, but I ain't got a pussy,' I told him.

'No – a posse, Luke. A group of a dozen honest men to catch a group of the evilest people you ever saw!' he said and he was sweating so much his armpits were stained black with the wet. He didn't smell too good neither.

'Oh, a posse!' I laughed. 'Where you going to find a dozen honest men in Cactus Rock?'

'I thought you might like to join, Luke,' he grinned. 'You're honest, aren't you?'

I was just going to tell him about the time I stole the bowl of the blind beggar on Main Street when my woman called, 'Bring him in, Luke!'

So I invited the sheriff in. We sat at the kitchen table and he told the terrible tale. 'We're after the Bender Family,' he said.

'That nice family that bought the shop and

saloon on Liberty Street?' I laughed when I thought of their lovely daughter Kate. 'Why that pretty girl Kate came here to tell our fortunes using carrot cards!'

'They're "tarot" cards,' my woman said. 'And I sent the girl packing. Don't know what her game was but she was up to no more good than a coyote in a hen-house.'

I was just going to argue when the sheriff cut in, 'Then you probably saved your husband's life, Mary!' (I never knew they called her Mary, I swear!)

'Shame,' she muttered.

Anyway the sheriff went on, 'Ma and Pa Bender came to town last summer with their son, Jake – a bit of a feeble-minded boy – and their daughter, Kate.'

'Not the only one that's feeble-minded round this town,' my woman muttered. I couldn't think who she meant, though I didn't like the way she looked at me.

'The Benders opened a shop and a saloon bar on Liberty Street and seemed to be doing good trade. But Kate went out every night, flirting with young strangers in town and taking them home!'

'Disgraceful,' my woman said and she gave one of those snooty sniffs up her nose that's longer than a vulture's beak.

'Trouble is,' the sheriff went on, 'those young men were never seen again.' He lowered his voice and slurped some coffee before he went on. 'One of the young men was followed by a friend when Kate took him to her home. The friend looked through a chink in the curtains and saw the young man sitting down to dinner. There was Ma Bender, Pa Bender and Kate sat at the table. There was no sign of the feeble-minded son.'

'Probably went to bed to rest his feeble head,' I said.

The sheriff ignored this common sense and continued, 'The young man had his back to a curtain. His friend saw Pa Bender give a signal with his hand. The curtain opened and the feeble-minded son stepped out. He had a heavy hammer in his hand!'

'Probably a loose nail in the floor,' I nodded.

'He brought the hammer down on the stranger's head! Crushed his skull to a pulp,' the sheriff hissed.

My woman groaned. 'Killers!' she sighed. 'Knew they were up to no good.'

'And robbers,' the sheriff added. 'They went through the stranger's pockets. Then they opened a trapdoor in the floor and dumped the body in the cellar. Naturally the stranger's friend came to tell me the terrible story of what he'd seen.'

'You arrested them?' my woman asked.

'I guess the young man must have made a noise when he saw what happened. He thinks he may have cried out. Whatever... By the time I got there the Benders had gone. We found the body in the cellar. This morning we dug in the yard and found another eleven bodies.'

'Sure glad they've gone!' I laughed. 'Town's a safer place.'

My woman scowled at me like a hog with indigestion. 'They have to be caught and brought to justice! You have to go after them, Luke. Help the sheriff catch them.'

I didn't like the sound of that. 'I don't know where they've gone!' I told her.

'No but you've got Old Blue!'

'Who's that?' I asked. I didn't remember having no friend called Old Blue.

'The dog,' she said. 'Only the finest Russian Bloodhound in the whole of Kansas ... if his power of smell hasn't been damaged by the stench of your feet,' she added.

And so Old Blue and me set off with the sheriff and a few other guys on the trail of the Bender family. And that's where the secret comes in. The dog tracked them ten miles to an old abandoned cabin near the border. It was nightfall by then and dark as a skunk's belly out there. The sheriff looked at the men and said, 'They're in that cabin, if this dog's nose is telling the truth!'

'Call them out,' one of the men said.

'Got to make sure they are the Benders,' I said. 'Someone needs to go and have a look.'

'Good thinking! You do it,' the sheriff said.

'Mo?'

'Yes. You look, Luke. If you took a look, Luke, we'd know.'

So they handed me a torch and lit it from a tinder box. I crept up to the window and that's when it all went wrong. There was no glass in the window, just an oiled cloth to keep out the draught. I tried to push the cloth to one side but I forgot I had the torch in my hand. In seconds the cloth caught fire and the wood cabin was ablaze. I ran.

We could all hear cries from inside the cabin, but they didn't last long. 'Aren't we going to save them?' I asked.

The sheriff shrugged. 'They'll only hang anyway. Best to let them fry, Luke.'

And that's what we did. Of course the governor of Kansas wouldn't like it. He'll say we took the law into our own hands and executed those Benders without a trial! So we went back to town and said we couldn't find them. We swore an oath to keep it all a secret.

But I told my woman, what's-her-name, and she wrote it all down here for me.

I solemnly swear that's the truth about the end of the Benders, brought to book and cooked by Luke Duke.

Signed with his mark,

The rumours said that the family had been caught and burnt alive. All members of the posse had then taken a vow of secrecy. Anything was possible in the wicked Wild West.

Wild West women

Women in the west were tough. They had to be. They were also given some pretty odd nicknames. Like…

Calamity Jane

Jane *said* her name came from fighting Indians, riding shotgun on stagecoaches, and so on... But really she got her name as a bar-room girl who smashed up saloons when she was drunk ... which was quite often!

'Calamity Jane' was born in 1848, and her real name was Martha Canary ... Canary? Wow, she must have been a bit of a tweet!

She often wore men's clothes and worked as a labourer. In 1875, she joined a US Army expedition against the Sioux Indians – as a male mule-skinner. She was discovered when she was caught swimming nude with mule drivers and thrown out!

In 1886, she was working in bars in Deadwood, where she spent the rest of her life. She died in 1903, of drink.

Nutty names

Calamity Jane is one of the most famous Wild West names …
but not the funniest!

Here are 10 more real ones. Can you fill in the blanks
with the women below to come up with the whole name?

1 Cowboy Queen ………   **6** Sad Story ………
2 Poker ………   **7** ……… the Pig
3 ……… Moustache   **8** ……… the Ton
4 Jolly ………   **9** Glass Eye ………
5 Diamond Tooth ………   **10** The Waddling ………

The last of the outlaw gangs

Butch Cassidy (real name George Leroy Parker) was born in Utah in 1866 and was robbing trains before he was 20. In 1889, Cassidy joined Tom McCarty to rob a bank in Denver. Inside the bank, McCarty held up a small bottle which he said contained high explosive...

The bank gave him $21,000 to go away. As he left the bank with the cash, he threw the bottle into a wastepaper basket. It was full of water. Ho! Ho!

Butch led the 'Hole in the Wall Gang', which later became the 'Wild Bunch'. A young cowboy joined who had already served term in jail in Sundance – so he got the name 'Sundance Kid'. But the gang wasn't as cheerful and harmless as they appear in the famous film about them.

These rustlers and robbers built cabins and corrals at the end of a desolate valley called Hole in the Wall, near Kaycee, Wyoming, which was a natural fortress with caves and a narrow entrance that was always guarded.

The gang weren't that bright. No one in the gang knew they had a private detective agent in their midst – Charles Siringo. He had joined the gang as an old, grizzled outlaw on the run for murder, and had been accepted without suspicion. He gathered enough information to spoil several planned robberies.

In 1898, posses were formed and $1,000 reward was offered for every 'Wild Bunch' outlaw dead or alive. Enraged, Butch and his chums went on the offensive, killing and burning farms. Then the USA declared war on Spain and attacked Spanish colonies. Butch offered the US government his gang and suggested the name 'The Wild Bunch Riders'. When the offer was rejected, Butch began robbing and killing again.

After one robbery, Butch and four chums bought city-slicker clothes and posed for a photo at Fort Worth. This photo was later used to identify gang members. But the gang's wild days were nearing an end. Gradually, gang members were caught and imprisoned, or killed, or just ran away.

Butch went by train and boat to South America, where Sundance and his girlfriend had already fled. In South America, they soon returned to robbing banks. Finally they were trapped by Bolivian soldiers. After a gunfight both Butch and Sundance were found dead. Had they been shot by the soldiers or had they killed themselves? Or maybe they'd had an argument? Something like...

Whatever happened, they were pretty much the last of the outlaw gangs.

THE TERRIBLE TWENTIETH CENTURY

In the twentieth century, America became one of the most powerful countries in the world. But as well as triumphs, there were disasters, and not everything was as happy and prosperous as it might have seemed...

Terrible twentieth-century timeline

1903 Orville and Wilbur Wright fly the first aeroplane. (Even though they invented it they can't spell it. They call it an 'airplane'.)

1914 World War I starts in Europe. The USA decides it doesn't want to join in just yet.

1917 Now, when it's nearly over, the USA joins in with all its men and machinery (on the winning side) and says, 'We won the war!'

1920 On 17 January, the USA goes 'dry'. For the next 13 years no US citizen has the 'legal' right to buy or sell alcoholic drinks. So it becomes an 'illegal' business run by gangsters.

1929 There is a 'crash' and many of the USA's biggest companies go broke. For the next ten years there will be a 'Depression' when the poor get poorer and suffer terribly.

1939 World War II starts in Europe. The USA decides it doesn't want to join in just yet.

1941 Now, when it's nearly over (well not quite), the USA joins in with all its men and machinery (on

WE INVENTED IT SO WE CAN CALL IT ANYTHING WE LIKE

IS HE OR WRIGHT?

OH SURE! HE'S FINE

I COULD KILL FOR A COLD BEER!

BAR

WE DO

WE'RE HAVING ANOTHER WAR, WOULD YOU LIKE TO COME?

NO THANKS

the winning side) and says, 'We won the war!' (Sound familiar?)

1945 USA invents the Atomic Bomb that can kill hundreds of thousands at a time. It's dropped on two Japanese cities and ends World War II.

1950s Russia and America fought together in World War II. Now they distrust and dislike one another. They have a 'Cold War' – lots of spying and threatening but no fighting. They also have a hot war where the USA tries to defend South Korea and smash the people of little North Korea.

1960s Now Russia and America have a race to put a man on the moon. The USA wins when Neil Armstrong jumps down on 20 July 1969. Meanwhile, back on earth, the USA is trying to defend the South Vietnamese government but is failing to smash the people of little North Vietnam.

The booze busters

In 1920 booze was banned in the USA (known as Prohibition). But it wasn't a sudden thing. Alcohol had been the most serious problem for the American people since slavery had been sorted with the Civil War. Now the battle against booze started another sort of war.

Bet you didn't know this intoxicating information…

1 In the 1700s and 1800s in the USA, liquor was seen as 'God's gift to mankind'. Rum was put into milk to send newborn babies to sleep! By the time most Americans were adults, they drank liquor every few hours.

2 The 'Old American Encyclopaedia' of 1830 said…

> In the Southern states it is the fashion to take a glass of whiskey, flavoured with mint, soon after waking. This is followed by more liquor at 11 o'clock, at lunch [whiskey and/or brandy], at 4 o'clock and throughout the evening.

Wow! Wonder what they did in their spare time?

3 Some of the worst drinkers were priests. They were given drink at every house they visited. Some clergy visited 20 houses each day. It was claimed in 1857 that half of all priests 'died drunkards'.

4 In the countryside drink was used as money. Prices in shops were shown in pints or gallons of whiskey and many shops gave favourite customers free drinks.

5 George Washington was famous for his drinking. As President he spent a quarter of his household expenses on booze.

6 In Georgia in 1734 strong drink was banned … but not beer. Nine years later they gave up trying to enforce this law. Most farmers had built their own alcohol factories and illegal booze was being smuggled across the border from South Carolina.

7 The word 'booze' comes from Edmund C Booze who stood for President in 1840. As he travelled across America looking for votes he sold his own brand of whiskey in bottles shaped like log cabins.

8 Drink smugglers were called 'bootleggers'. This was because illegal drink was hidden in the tops of smugglers' oversized boots. When Georgia bootleggers were caught in the 1730s the juries set them free because if they'd locked up every bootlegger there wouldn't be enough jails. Pity the lesson of Georgia was not remembered in the 1920s.

9 Soon scientists and doctors were claiming that liquor was the cause of everything from rheumatism to old age. One myth claimed that drunkards could 'spontaneously combust' – that is they could suddenly burst into flames.

10 The Civil War drove men to drink so they could face the horrors. But after the war the Ban-the-booze groups began to grow again. One women's group persuaded schools to teach 'The Evils of Drink'. How did teachers do this? With a cheerful little experiment…

There's no booziness like show booziness

It was no use telling a drunk, 'You have to stop drinking otherwise you'll end up roasting in Hell!' For a start he'd be too drunk to care! And, for another thing, he might look forward to seeing all his pickled friends down there! So what the booze-busters had to do was make the drunkards ASHAMED of their hobby. They had to show the effect that drink had on their wives and children.

The best way to get these messages across was often in songs that could be sung all over the country – radio and television hadn't been invented. The top pop songs of the late 1800s were about the evils of drunkenness.

These songs were full of misery and suffering and pathetic women and children. They were also pathetic songs. If you had one of these sung to you you'd either **a)** throw up, **b)** burst into tears, or **c)** have a drink of whiskey to drown the misery.

In America the 'Ban Drink Campaign', the Temperance Movement, was helped by the theatres where you could go and hear terrible tales of drunkenness.

Now, thanks to *Horrible Histories,* you can find out for yourself the miseries of drink! After visiting 'Doctor Dreary's Temperance Show' you may never drink again … not even water! Step inside…

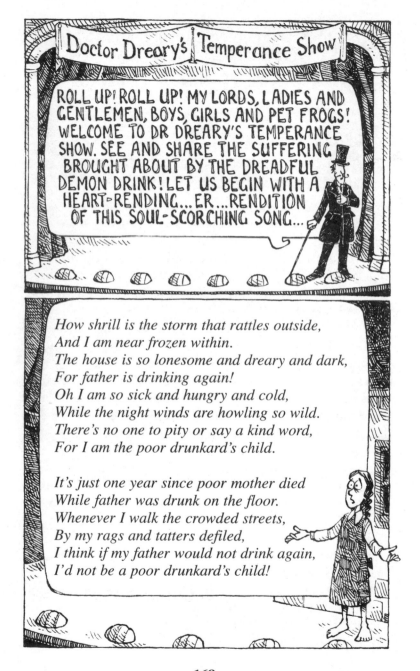

ROLL UP! ROLL UP! MY LORDS, LADIES AND GENTLEMEN, BOYS, GIRLS AND PET FROGS! WELCOME TO DR DREARY'S TEMPERANCE SHOW. SEE AND SHARE THE SUFFERING BROUGHT ABOUT BY THE DREADFUL DEMON DRINK! LET US BEGIN WITH A HEART-RENDING... ER... RENDITION OF THIS SOUL-SCORCHING SONG...

How shrill is the storm that rattles outside,
And I am near frozen within.
The house is so lonesome and dreary and dark,
For father is drinking again!
Oh I am so sick and hungry and cold,
While the night winds are howling so wild.
There's no one to pity or say a kind word,
For I am the poor drunkard's child.

It's just one year since poor mother died
While father was drunk on the floor.
Whenever I walk the crowded streets,
By my rags and tatters defiled,
I think if my father would not drink again,
I'd not be a poor drunkard's child!

VERY SAD DEAR, BUT THERE ARE STILL SOME BEER-SOAKED BRUTES OUT THERE IN THE AUDIENCE WHO ARE NOT GOING TO GIVE UP SATAN'S SHANDY! SO HERE WE HAVE THE FAMOUS DOCTOR, BENJAMIN RUSH, WRITER OF THE POPULAR BOOK, 'AN INQUIRY INTO THE EFFECT OF SPIRITUOUS LIQUORS ON THE HUMAN BODY AND MIND'*

I HAVE PRODUCED A CHART SHOWING THE DECLINE OF THE DRUNKARD THAT SHOWS THAT DRINK LEADS TO SIN, SIN LEADS TO DISEASE AND DISEASE LEADS TO SUFFERING.

~ THE DECLINE OF THE DRUNKARD ~

The drink...	the sin...	the disease..	the suffering
punch.....	idleness....	sickness....	debt
egg rum ...	gambling...	hand tremors.	jail
brandy....	fighting....	red nose....	black eyes
hot beer....	swearing...	sore legs...	poor house
strong beer..	stealing....	yellow skin..	local prison
spirits in morning....	lying......	swollen body.	state prison
spirits all day.	burglary....	fits.....	prison for life
spirits day and night...	murder.....	madness...	HANGING!

*A hugely popular book in 1785. Rush's book became a US best-seller. Though in Washington, President James Madison continued to drink one pint of whiskey before breakfast!

169

SO YOU SEE HOW DRINKING CAN LEAD TO YOU BEING HANGED! YOU CAN ALWAYS TELL A DRUNKARD! HE BEGINS BY SINGING, THEN ROARING, THEN IMITATING THE NOISES OF ANIMALS, THEN JUMPING, THEN TEARING OFF THE CLOTHES AND ENDS BY DANCING NAKED

IT'S A BIT LIKE WHEN YOU EAT TOO MANY SCHOOL DINNERS, EH KIDS? ANYWAY THANK YOU DR RUSH. NOW LET'S HAVE ANOTHER OF THOSE CHARMING SONGS FROM THE WISTFUL WARBLER, LITTLE BESSIE

1. Out in the gloomy night sadly I roam.
2. Father's a drunkard and mother is dead.
3. No one now cares for me, no one would cry,
4. Weary and tired I've been wandering all day,
5. All the day long I've been begging for bread,
6. I have no mother dear, no pleasant home.
7. Asking for work but I'm too small they say!
8. Even if poor little Bessie should die!

OOOOPS! LITTLE BESSIE'S BEEN AT THE GINGER BEER! SHE GOT THE FIRST LINE RIGHT... BUT THE REST ARE MIXED UP! CAN YOU HELP HER BY PUTTING THEM IN THE RIGHT ORDER?

Answer: 1, 6, 3, 8, 4, 7, 5, 2

Carry Nation's Street

The most famous fighter against drink was probably Carry Nation. If television had been around in the early 1900s they may have told her story like this...

Beat that booze ban!

The US people were so upset by these stories of dangerous drink that in the end they banned it. On 17 January 1920 it became illegal to buy alcohol ... unless it was medicine from a doctor or wine used in church.

But most people still wanted to drink. What would you do to beat the ban? Many people stocked up huge amounts of booze before the ban began. But once it started there were millions who dodged the law to drink ... or to make a lot of money.

Here are ten tips from the people who did it...

175

In Chicago, one hour after midnight on 17 January 1920, masked gunmen stole $100,000 of 'medicinal' whiskey from a whiskey factory. The first of hundreds of gangster attacks in the battle against the booze ban.

Fake 'Sweet Whiskey' was made from ether, mixed with nitric and sulphuric acids. Don't spill it on your clothes! Chicago's 'Yack-Yack Whiskey' was made from iodine and burnt sugar. Yuck! Yuck! From Mexico came 'American Whiskey' made from potatoes and cactus – ouch!

More booze was smuggled in but not all smugglers were male. Spanish Marie smuggled booze on her boat *Kid Boots*. She had a revolver strapped to her waist, a knife stuck in her belt and wore a red bandanna tied around her head.

In New York in 1927, there were 30,000 Speakeasy bars – twice as many bars as before Prohibition!

177

Losers and winners

The rich people, the politicians, the police and the gangsters enjoyed their drink and made huge profits from Prohibition. Of course it was the poor who suffered as usual. Poor Fred Palm got a life sentence for having a pint of gin. So did a mother of ten in Michigan. But not all the police raids were a success.

Which just goes to show ... you shouldn't spend a dollar when a woman spends a penny.

In December 1932 the Prohibition law was dropped. One year later, the last State, Utah, went 'wet'. Across the USA there were parades and torchlight processions. Prohibition was dead. So were tens of thousands of people who'd drunk fake and poisonous booze. Hundreds died in the gang wars and thousands went blind from the effects of the drink. Prohibition was not one of the USA's cleverest ideas!

Happy Valentine's Day, you guys!

Prohibition meant big money for the men who sold the illegal booze. But they had to protect the money with some pretty violent men. One of the most vicious gang leaders was Big Al Capone who sold booze in Chicago. And it didn't pay to upset Big Al.

One man who tried to steal Capone's business was 'Bugs' Moran. Al Capone set up a very special Valentine's Day gift for 'Bugs', then Al went on holiday to Florida. The amazing thing about the story was the way it appeared in the newspapers the next day!

179

The Chicago Herald

COPS CHOP BUGS BOYS

Last night seven members of the Bugs Moran gang died in a hail of machine-gun bullets. On St Valentine's Day, last night, the men arrived at a warehouse in Clarke Street to wait for a truckload of stolen whiskey. But there was no whiskey – only death in a police trap.

A local resident, Andy Reiss, described the scene: 'I heard a truck door slam and looked out of my window opposite the warehouse. I saw two cops in uniform and two plain-clothes detectives get out of a police wagon.

They ran into the warehouse. That's when I heard a sound like a pneumatic drill – I guess that was the machine-gun! Then the two uniformed cops came out with their guns pointed at two other men. It all went quiet for a while then we heard the guard dog begin to howl. It didn't stop so we went across to investigate.'

Reiss's neighbour (who did not wish to give his name) said, 'The door was open so we went in. It was like a slaughterhouse in there. There were seven bodies. The cops had just lined them up against the wall and blasted them. The blood was flooding over the floor and into the drain. The only sound was one guy moaning. We went and called for an ambulance but it was too late for him. It's a bit of a shock to think the police can murder men in cold blood like that!'

The neighbour's wife added, 'Moran's gang stole booze from a police gang two weeks ago. Bet ya this was their revenge!'

The police chief denies that the Chicago police force had anything to do with the massacre.

Our reporter tracked down 'Bugs' Moran to his home today. Moran agreed the men were members of his gang but insisted, 'That was meant to be me in there! I stopped off for a cup of coffee so I was late. I saw the police run in and I escaped with my life. But I thought it was just an ordinary raid! I just can't believe the police would do this to my boys. We pay the cops too well. Only Capone kills like that!' The investigation continues.

Al Capone – involved?

The newspapers got some of the facts right but one important one wrong ... the killers were NOT the Chicago police. They were Al Capone's gang dressed up as police. They fooled their victims, who lined up against the wall to be searched, and they fooled the witnesses.

The four killers were never punished for the St Valentine's Day massacre, but two died horribly anyway. These two, Anesimi and Scalise, agreed to turn on their boss, Al Capone, and kill him. Big Al heard about their plot and planned a suitable revenge. Capone arranged a big dinner party where Anesimi and Scalise were the main guests. Al gave a speech and talked about how important it was to be loyal to your boss. Then he had Anesimi and Scalise tied to their chairs. He took out a baseball bat and, in front of his guests, battered the heads of the traitors till they were dead.

If that's not enough to put you off your dinner, what is?

Kool killers

Prohibition was great for gangsters who made pots of money selling booze. But America has always been great at creating crooks and murderers. Here are five of US history's most foul...

Name: Lizzie Borden

Dates: 1893, Fall River, Massachusetts

Crime: Accused of trying to poison her family. When that failed she was said to have chopped her sleeping mother up with an axe. She then waited for her father to come home and she chopped him up too!

Notes: She got away with it! The jury didn't want to see a posh young lady hang so they found her 'Not Guilty'. But American kids had no doubt she did it and enjoyed the song:
    Lizzie Borden took an axe,
    And gave her mother forty whacks.
    When she saw what she had done
    She gave her father forty-one!

Name: The Axeman of New Orleans

Dates: 1911–19, New Orleans

Crime: In 1911 he broke into six Italian grocery shops and killed the Italian grocers and their wives. Went quiet for a few years then struck again in 1918 and 1919.

Notes: Never caught. The widow of one of his victims shot a man and said he was the Axeman. She could have been right because he was never heard of again. But the people of New Orleans enjoyed the horror – they had 'Axeman parties' where everyone went dressed as Italian grocers and axemen! There was even a popular song called "The Mysterious Axeman's Jazz".

Name: The Barker Family

Dates: 1930s, Missouri

Crime: The gang, led by Big Bad Ma Barker, robbed banks and killed anyone who got in the way. But they made better money by kidnapping rich people. That's the way they made $3 million.

Notes: When the police tracked Ma Barker to her hideout they attacked with tear-gas and machine-guns. She was found dead, still clutching her machine-gun. Tough cookie. Her son Lloyd was released from prison in 1947 after serving 25 years. He went home to his loving wife – who killed him! Another tough lady!

Name: John Dillinger

Dates: 1930s, Chicago

Crime: Bank robber. He was so good at it the Chicago police formed a special 'Dillinger Squad' of 40 men. The head of the FBI labelled him 'Public Enemy Number One' – well, it's always nice to be number one at something.

Notes: He was captured in Arizona but escaped using a wooden 'gun' blackened with shoe polish. (When two of his gang tried to escape with a gun made of soap, they failed ... you'd have thought they'd have got clean away, wouldn't you?) A $10,000 dollar reward was offered for his capture – dead or alive – and his loving girlfriend told the police where to find him. He was shot dead. There were stories that the dead man was a 'double' for Dillinger and that the real gangster lived on. Not very likely.

Name: Bonnie Parker and Clyde Barrow

Dates: 1930s, Texas

Crime: Stealing cars to carry out robberies with violence – LOTS of violence.

Notes: Bonnie and Clyde's first big robbery went wrong when the getaway car broke down and they had to escape on mules! Their adventures were sensational news in America and they were very popular, even though they murdered at least 12 people! They helped some convicts to escape – then one convict betrayed them to the police. (Trust no one in the crime game.) They were finally caught in a police ambush and machine-gunned to death. They were buried in separate cemeteries even though they'd asked to be buried together. Bonnie even wrote a poem about it – such a bad poem she deserved to be shot for it...

Some day they will go down together,
And they will bury them side by side.
To a few it means grief,
To the law it's relief,
But it's death to Bonnie and Clyde.

The rabid racists

The cruel Ku Klux Klan (KKK) was formed in 1866 after the Civil War had freed the slaves. The KKK members (mostly men) wanted to go back to the 'good old days' when whites were bosses and blacks were slaves. They would do this by making life miserable for black people. (You and I spell 'Clan' with a 'C'. But these racists were thicker than cold treacle and couldn't even spell the name of their klub!)

It was against the law to be a member of the KKK so the murdering members wore silly pointy hats to hide their faces. Sadly there was nothing silly about their hobby.

A typical terror tale

In 1934 an old ex-slave told this story...

I was in a group of freed slaves who set off looking for work. Then the Ku Klux Klan came after us so we hid in the woods. All we had to eat were a few biscuits. We broke up one of the biscuits and scattered it on the forest trail as bait to catch racoons. One of our group, Austin Saunders, was caught by a Klan patrol.

'What are you doing?' they asked.

'Leaving bait for racoons,' he told them.

'We'll help you!' they laughed.

They shot poor Austin and left his body in the middle of the trail. They took his last biscuit and stuck it in his mouth. 'There you are! Bait for racoons!'

Postcards from Hell

Governments can pass laws. Groups like the KKK can be banned. But laws and bans can't always change the cruelty in people's hearts. A hundred years after slavery was stopped there were still people punishing black people for simply being black!

This makes as much sense as your teacher punishing you if your name is Mary or George because your teacher has decided to hate all Marys and Georges!

In May 2000 a collection of postcards were put on display in New York. They were all photographs of black people being 'lynched' – that is hanged by a mob without any sort of trial.

Some of the black victims' crimes were as simple as not showing their racist killers 'enough respect'. The victims were often whipped or cut up or burned before or while they were dying, just to add to the suffering.

In 1916 in Texas a 17-year-old black boy was accused of murder. A white mob got him before the police and began by cutting off his ears. They then fastened him by a chain and began to roast him over a fire. When he tried to climb the chain to escape they cut off his fingers. The scene was turned into a postcard. On the back of the postcard was a message from one of the torturers to his family...

Ma and Pa! this is the barbecue we had last night! Your son, Joe

The postcards didn't just show the victim. They showed the large crowds that gathered to watch the hangings like some sort of sport.

The earliest postcards were from the 1880s – that's nasty. But the later ones are from 1968 – that's scary.

Did you know…?

Of course some racists were too impatient to bother with lynchings. In Tulsa, Oklahoma, in 1921 a group of white men flew over a black area of the town and dropped dynamite on to the houses. Over one thousand homes were wrecked and 75 men, women and children died.

Stop that lynching

What did the US government do to stop lynchings? Not a lot. Oh, they *talked* about it of course. When several Italians were lynched in New Orleans for making friends with black people, President Theodore Roosevelt *said*…

This is a despicable crime!

But he *wrote* to his sister…

Actually I think the lynching of the Italians was rather a good thing!

No wonder it went on so long when Presidents supported the criminals.

Is it finally all over at last? Not completely. The hangman's noose is still a sign of hatred in the USA – anyone caught threatening someone with a noose could get ten years in prison. But that doesn't stop some people. Black people in 2000 have had to put up with…

- Nooses hanging from the door to their work room.
- Nooses drawn around photos of their children.
- Nooses waved under their noses while people taunt, 'This is what we used to do to you!'

The Ku Klux Klan would be proud of them!

In 1963 Martin Luther King, the most famous leader for black American civil rights, declared...

I have a dream that one day on the red hills of Georgia, sons of former slaves and the sons of former slave owners will be able to sit down together at the table of brotherhood.

Just five years later King was assassinated. Will his dream ever come true?

EPILOGUE

The history of the USA is horrible. It began with Americans crushing the native Indians to take over their land.

General William Tecumseh Sherman of the US Army had a simple little mind and a simple answer to the Indians...

The more Indians we can kill this year, the less will have to be killed next year. The more I see of these Indians, the more sure I am they all have to be killed.

(The Indians didn't think much of him either.)

The problem wasn't that a beanbag-brained general said this. The problem was so many Americans agreed with him!

By 1845 they had decided they had a 'Manifest Destiny' to take over the whole continent of America. They smashed the Mexicans out of their way and got what they wanted.

Were they satisfied? No. By the twentieth century they wanted to be: 'the greatest country on the face of this earth'! The trouble is the people who stood in the way of US 'greatness' usually got seriously hurt.

In 1901 the USA wanted to take over the Philippines. General Jacob Smith told his US soldiers...

Kill and burn! And the more you kill and burn the more you will please me!

He wanted no prisoners and he thought anyone over the age of ten years could be a rebel and should suffer. The US troops killed and burned with the usual excuse...

I WAS JUST FOLLOWING ORDERS

In the Second World War, the Americans wanted to finish the war with the Japanese enemy. The answer? An atomic-bomb massacre. As General Sherman might have said, 'The more Japanese you kill in 1945 the less you'll have to kill in 1946.' Women and children? Sad, but if they get in the way they'll get hurt!

Even in 1968, US soldiers in Vietnam attacked a village, looking for enemy warriors but killing women, old people and children when they got in the way. The US troops were brought by helicopter in to the village known as My Lai 4 and they lashed out at everyone they found – 347 women, children and old men. No soldiers. No one to fight back. Tough troops, eh? Some villagers were herded into ditches, where they were shot. An army photographer took pictures of those bodies dumped in ditches.

Does that sound just like the Sand Creek Indian massacre of 104 years before? Or the massacre in King Philips's War 200 years before that?

The officer in charge at My Lai, William Calley, said the massacre was, 'No big deal.'

The mother of one of the US killers said...

I sent the US Army a good boy and they turned him into a murderer.

Hopefully the Americans have finally learned the lessons of their history. Hopefully there will be no more Sand Creeks or My Lais in the 21st century.

Hopefully. But who can tell? After all, history has been horrible in the past. Will it be horrible in the future too?

Now why not visit www.terry-deary.com